T0277180

## A GREAT COCKTAIL IS MORE THAN A DRINK. IT'S A MULTISENSORY CELEBRATION.

So indulge yourself. Find yourself transported to a tropical getaway or a quiet rural retreat as you sip on a fruity, rum-soaked Per My Last Email or a Front Porch Swing (a delightfully countrified Manhattan). Wax nostalgic while enjoying an Afternoon Snack (a grown-up riff on ants on a log). Drink in the essence of late summer with the Smoked Corn Silk Old Fashioned. And to complete the spread in style, pair with any of the inspired seasonal small plates or modernized bar snacks, from blistered peppers with a creamy walnut sauce to Sichuan-spiced popcorn.

Whether your goal is to dazzle friends or simply to relax with a well-deserved nightcap, *The Vedge Bar Book* will help you turn cocktail hour into an experience truly worth savoring.

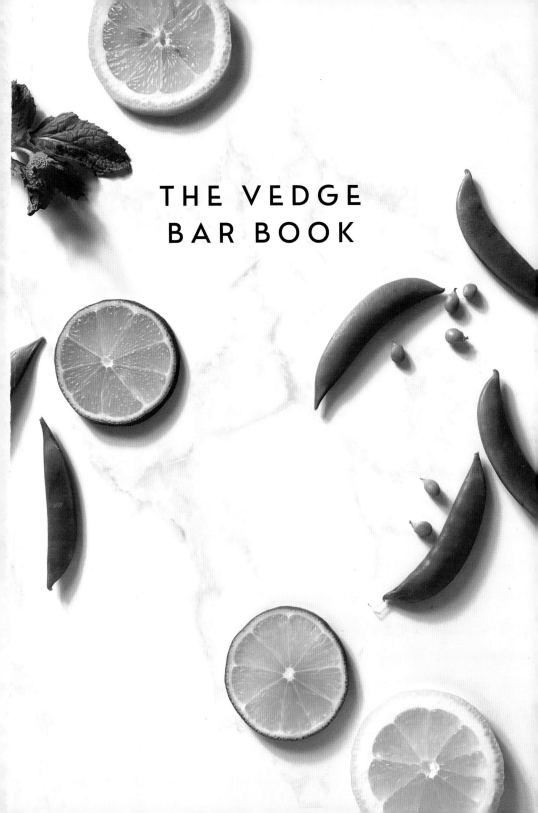

# THE VEDGE
# BAR BOOK

ALSO BY
KATE JACOBY AND
RICH LANDAU

*Vedge*

*V Street*

*To Rich's dad, Mike Landau,*
*who was our biggest fan*
—Rich and Kate

*To Amanda, my love for always*
—Brian

*To my grandmother, for always*
*supporting me*
—Ginevra

# THE VEDGE BAR BOOK

*Plant-Based Cocktails and Light Bites for Inspired Entertaining*

## KATE JACOBY AND RICH LANDAU

### with Brian Bolles and Ginevra Reiff

#### PHOTOGRAPHY BY TED NGHIEM

THE EXPERIMENT

NEW YORK

THE VEDGE BAR BOOK: *Plant-Based Cocktails and Light Bites for Inspired Entertaining*
Copyright © 2024 by Kate Jacoby and Rich Landau
Photographs, including cover and author photographs, copyright © 2024 by Ted Nghiem

All rights reserved. Except for brief passages quoted in newspaper, magazine, radio, television, or online reviews, no portion of this book may be reproduced, distributed, or transmitted in any form or by any means, electronic or mechanical, including photocopying, recording, or information storage or retrieval system, without the prior written permission of the publisher.

The Experiment, LLC
220 East 23rd Street, Suite 600
New York, NY 10010-4658
theexperimentpublishing.com

THE EXPERIMENT and its colophon are registered trademarks of The Experiment, LLC. Many of the designations used by manufacturers and sellers to distinguish their products are claimed as trademarks. Where those designations appear in this book and The Experiment was aware of a trademark claim, the designations have been capitalized.

The Experiment's books are available at special discounts when purchased in bulk for premiums and sales promotions as well as for fund-raising or educational use. For details, contact us at info@theexperimentpublishing.com.

Library of Congress Cataloging-in-Publication

Names: Landau, Rich, 1967-, author. | Jacoby, Kate, 1980- author. | Bolles, Brian, author. | Reiff, Ginevra, author.
Title: The Vedge Bar book : plant-based cocktails and light bites for inspired entertaining / Kate Jacoby and Rich Landau with Brian Bolles and Ginevra Reiff ; photography by Ted Nghiem.
Description: New York : The Experiment, [2024] | Includes index.
Identifiers: LCCN 2024026698 (print) | LCCN 2024026699 (ebook) | ISBN 9798893030143 | ISBN 9798893030150 (ebook)
Subjects: LCSH: Vedge Bar. | Cocktails. | Snack foods. | LCGFT: Cookbooks.
Classification: LCC TX951 .L323 2024 (print) | LCC TX951 (ebook) | DDC 641.8--dc23/eng/20240627
LC record available at https://lccn.loc.gov/2024026698
LC ebook record available at https://lccn.loc.gov/2024026699

ISBN 979-8-89303-014-3
Ebook ISBN 979-8-89303-015-0

Cover and text design, and photograph on page i, by Beth Bugler

Manufactured in China

First printing November 2024
10 9 8 7 6 5 4 3 2 1

# CONTENTS

# INTRODUCTION

artini, please," Norman Paperman says at the bar of the Gull Reef Club in Herman Wouk's novel *Don't Stop the Carnival.* "Bombay gin. Boissière vermouth, two to one. Lemon peel. Chill the glass, please."

On our very first trip as a couple, Rich read to Kate this passage, a longtime favorite of his. We then looked at each other and said, "Let's find that bar and live that moment."

The book was written in the '50s, an era when drinks were simple but the whole experience of drinking had an air of glamour. Cocktail hour meant a white-suited bartender, live piano, beautiful glassware, and stylish people. It was an occasion for celebrating, a chance to unwind from a hard day or to get ready for a festive night ahead.

The idea of finding our own Gull Reef Club has stuck with both of us for decades now. Sipping an elegant cocktail at the perfect bar on a perfect night: It's an experience we've sought at bars all over the world—and it's the feeling we always strive to create at our own restaurants.

In the '90s, before Rich became a chef, he was a bartender. In those days, the cocktails being served were a far cry from Mr. Paperman's martini. The liqueurs we slung were a rogues' gallery of sweet Midori, syrupy peach schnapps, and Chambord—sloshy messes masking cheap vodka and rum on a shortcut to a hangover. Rich remembers those drinks with equal parts nostalgia and nausea. The electric colors, artificial juices, and soda guns still haunt him to this day.

But how far we've come since then.

When we got our first liquor license in 2006, Kate instantly set about realizing her vision for what a bar in this new century should look like: artisanal craft spirits, a groundbreaking natural wine list, cocktails made with fresh vegetable and fruit infusions, tinctures and bitters. From day one, the mission of Vedge's bar program has been to give as much consideration to our wine list and cocktails as we do to the food we cook and plate on a nightly basis. We like our drinks sophisticated, honoring the pristine flavors of quality local ingredients, yet with an element of whimsy and fun—and often featuring a seasonal vegetable or two.

Our beverage program has also been shaped by each of the talented people who've taken their place behind the bar over the years. We are honored to be working with such talent, including our coauthors, Brian and Ginevra, who've helped take Vedge's beverage program—and our hospitality in general—to amazing new heights. And we're elated to share our recipes—some of the most beloved sips and snacks to have made it onto our bar menu over the past decade-plus—with you.

At Vedge, our bar staff spends anywhere from two to four hours each day making syrups, infusions, mixtures, and garnishes, before we even touch a shaker or look at a piece of ice. We don't expect you to go to quite those lengths. (After all, even hosting the most well-attended cocktail party probably won't require you to whip up dozens upon dozens of drinks over the course of the night, as we do at the restaurant! And if you're expecting a crowd, we recommend serving one of our batched cocktails so you can join in the fun.) But most of our recipes do call for some advance prep, because we believe a memorable cocktail takes time to do right. Just stay organized and plan ahead; we promise the results are worth it.

These days, we still get a thrill out of traveling in search of a cocktail that will make us feel as though we've been transported into the pages of *Don't Stop the Carnival*. And we've discovered plenty that have come damn close, from some of the world's most iconic bars—the Long Bar at Raffles in Singapore, Sloppy Joe's in Key West, the New York Bar in Tokyo—as well as from unassuming beach bars, pubs, dives, and hotel bars. Thanks to a talented new generation of bartenders, we're living in a new golden age of craft cocktails.

So while we'll never stop searching for that mythical "bar at the end of the world," we'll be sure to appreciate every delicious sip along the way—and to do our best to create our own version at Vedge. Perhaps one of our patrons will go on to write a line or two about one of our cocktails, and years from now, a future generation will read it and dream of having been there.

Cocktail culture is having its moment, and it's a great time to drink it all in.

—Kate and Rich

# OUR TAKE ON SPIRITS

Whether you are a novice bartender or you keep a curated collection of whiskies on a decked-out bar cart, we figure it's helpful to share some context about our spirit selection at Vedge. These notes are meant to give a brief overview of common spirits and our preferences, as our recipes are often designed with specific bottles in mind.

## VODKA

Vodka is a clear and essentially flavorless spirit that was popularized in Eastern Europe. It's now made the world over from countless different ingredients: wheat, corn, potato, grape, beet—basically any source of sugar. Often boasting multiple distillations, vodka is prized for its purity. Most brands work well in all recipes, although premium brands may feel less fiery on the palate. Our favorite is a potato vodka from Poland called Luksusowa.

## GIN

Gin is a distillate made in much the same way as vodka, with purity being key. Juniper is an essential component, but beyond that, additions like rose hip, citrus peel, peppercorn, lavender, and others can play a part in achieving a particular gin's distinctive flavor profile. There are several different styles of gin, from high-proof Navy Strength to sweeter varieties like Old Tom. Beefeater London Dry is a solid, versatile choice.

## RUM

Rum is a spirit distilled from sugarcane. Often miscategorized by color rather than region or place of origin, rum is an extremely varied category. Most rum is made from distilled molasses. Others use fresh-pressed sugarcane juice and boast a distinct grassy note. Industrialization has left its mark on rum; a lot of distilleries use stories-tall column stills to produce clean and neutral-tasting rum. But there are also traditionalists who use decades- (if not centuries-) old copper pot stills and age their rum in familial oak vats to maintain that rich, funky, fruity character. A light rum like Plantation 3 Stars covers most of our mixing needs.

## AGAVE-DERIVED SPIRITS

**Tequila,** made from fermented blue agave, is a Mexican spirit produced predominantly in the state of Jalisco. Blanco tequila is clear, its flavor young and fresh. Reposado tequila has rested for up to one year in wooden barrels, giving it a richer body and more savory notes. Añejo tequila is aged at least one to three years, resulting in a smooth and complex spirit that can be enjoyed solo. Joven tequila blends Blanco and Reposado, each blend uniquely bridging the two distinct flavor profiles. Any 100-percent agave tequila will be great for use with the recipes in this book, but we prefer Libélula Joven tequila.

**Mezcal** is a broader term than tequila for agave-derived spirits, applied to spirits made from a wide range of agave and originating from a much larger geographic area in Mexico. Another key difference occurs before distillation.

To make tequila, agaves are roasted in either large brick ovens or gigantic metal pressure cookers called autoclaves. To make mezcal, agaves are traditionally roasted in a stone-lined pit alongside smoldering local woods, resulting in a pronounced smoky flavor. The looser restrictions on general mezcal-making means mezcal comes in a broad range of styles. Our go-to in this book is Banhez Ensamble, a clear and bright option made from Espadín and Barril agave.

## WHISKEY

**Scotch** comes strictly from Scotland, must be aged at least three years, and often has a smoky flavor that's achieved by burning peat during the malting process. Scotch is categorized by the five geographic regions in which it's made. You can find both single malts and blends, the former indicating that the Scotch was produced in a single distillery, the latter that it was made with a combination of Scotches from multiple distilleries, which often makes blends more affordable than single malts. Famous Grouse is a blended Scotch that adds a malty flavor and just the right amount of smoke.

**Irish whiskey,** like Scotch, is made from fermented grain and aged for at least three years, but Irish distillers incorporate a slightly broader range of grains and tend to favor a triple-distillation process. The result is a smoother style that's excellent for sipping on its own, with or without ice. It's also a surprisingly versatile cocktail ingredient, with Powers being a great choice in most mixes.

**Bourbon** is an aged spirit made from corn and primarily produced in Kentucky. To be called a bourbon, a liquor needs to be made up of no less than 51 percent corn, aged at least three months, and produced somewhere in the US. Labels reading "straight" or "bottled in bond" denote longer aging, at least two or four years respectively. A "cask strength" label indicates a higher proof, with a greater concentration of both alcohol and flavor. Wild Turkey 101 is a high-proof option that adds great alcoholic intensity to a drink.

American **rye** has many parallels to bourbon. It's an aged spirit with roots in the Mid-Atlantic region, made from at least 51 percent rye grain and aged in new, charred American oak barrels. Rye is often prized for its dry, slightly savory flavor, and some ryes can be a bit salty or spicy. It almost disappeared entirely during Prohibition, but with renewed interest in recent years, styles of rye whiskey have become quite varied, including 80-proof and high-proof styles, just like bourbon. Rittenhouse is a great option for everyday use.

**Japanese whiskey,** originally developed to emulate Scotch, has its own distinct character thanks to being made in column stills and is often aged in barrels made mostly from native Japanese oak. You can find a wide range of single malt and blended Japanese whiskies to enjoy as you would any other whiskey. For cocktails, we like Suntory's Toki for its smoothness and lightly spiced flavor.

## BRANDY

With origins in medieval France, brandy is the outcome of aging distilled wine. The practice became widely adopted for many reasons, including taste preferences, shipping convenience, and even avoiding tax burdens, as the concentrated liquor requires less space to store. Wine-making regions around the world specialize in specific styles, with renowned examples like French cognac or South American pisco. Of course, wine can be made from fruits other than grapes, so we also have apple-based French Calvados and American apple brandy, also known as applejack. And variations like eau de vie or grappa utilize other fruits or byproducts of winemaking. Brandy is often enjoyed as an after-dinner digestif. When worked into cocktails, it's a terrific base spirit offering rich flavor and a robust mouthfeel.

## LIQUEUR

Think of liqueur as an exaggerated gin. It's a spirit that has been flavored, then often heavily sweetened, to achieve a singular character. The flavor can be highly focused, like a peach schnapps, or it might represent a brand's coveted secret recipe, as in Green Chartreuse. Some forgo liqueur's typical sweetness to concentrate on a range of bitter flavors like you'd find in amari. Because the limitless options all have their own distinct flavors, you should always use the exact type of liqueur that's called for in a recipe. Some liqueurs, like orange, might have a range of viable options (like Cointreau, Grand Marnier, or generic triple sec), but with others (like Campari), the brand-specific formula will drive the whole drink!

## BITTERS

Bitters are made by infusing a high-proof spirit with a selection of bitter roots and botanicals. We've had success designing small-batch bitters for some specific cocktails, but because the flavor profiles vary greatly between brands, it's best to use the specific brand called for in a recipe—often Angostura or Peychaud's. And always pay close attention to the amount called for because a little goes a long way.

## WINE

Wine shows up in many classic cocktails, from prosecco in a Bellini to champagne topping a Kir Royale. Tempranillo forms the base of Spain's famous sangria, but it can also be added to cocktails, like the float in a New York Sour. Whether a recipe calls for a sweet dessert wine or a fortified wine like an aromatized vermouth, it's important to understand what that ingredient is doing in the cocktail before you consider making any substitutions. And if you must deviate, do so with careful intention.

# ESSENTIAL INGREDIENTS

Beyond spirits, many other ingredients are just as important to the success of our recipes and benefit from some added context. Understanding what each ingredient contributes to the finished cocktail is key to becoming a better home bartender.

## SUGAR

We use organic granulated cane sugar behind our bar. It's a little coarser than processed white sugar (which actually comes from beets), and it carries a tiny bit more molasses flavor, but it dissolves and caramelizes just like white sugar. When we want more pronounced notes of molasses and baking spice, we turn to demerara, a raw cane sugar with a crunchy texture.

## SIMPLE SYRUP

Simple syrup is basically liquid sugar—not a thick, burnt sugar caramel, but more like sugar water. A good simple syrup adds concentrated, clean-tasting sweetness that balances a drink's acidity or bitterness. In our cocktails, we often use flavored simple syrups to showcase other flavors and infuse them into drinks. Subtle differences in our syrup recipes are always intentional; some call for fruit or vegetable juices rather than water, while others need careful straining, so be sure to follow each recipe as written.

### SIMPLE SYRUP
Makes about 2 cups (480 ml)

**2½ cups (500 g) sugar**

**2 cups (480 ml) hot, not boiling, water**

**1 teaspoon salt**

Combine all the ingredients in a bowl and stir until the sugar is dissolved. Let cool completely, then store in an airtight container in the fridge for up to 2 weeks.

## OTHER SYRUPS

Other sweet syrups can also add nuance to drinks, like the floral agave or the subtle smokiness of hickory syrup. Just be mindful of their texture. Some, like maple, dissolve nicely in a shaker, but others, like brown rice syrup or coconut syrup, can be super thick and sticky, requiring dilution with another liquid ingredient before mixing.

## FRUIT

While it's true that many fruits are sweet, in cocktails, we focus on the flavor and texture that different fruits provide, considering any residual sugar secondarily. It's also important to think about whether your fruit ingredients are fresh, frozen, dried, or preserved. In our recipes, we're clear about when to use fresh fruit and when it's better to use frozen or preserved.

## CITRUS

Just like other fruits aren't purely sweet, citrus is not just tart. Sure, fresh lemon juice is a bar staple because it helps balance flavors and make a drink pop. But citrus fruits are diverse and offer a range of ways to pack your drink with flavor. Some oranges are sour; some grapefruits are sweet. Key limes have a uniquely floral quality, as do Meyer lemons and yuzu. Bergamot can be downright bitter. Oftentimes, fresh juice is best, but citrus peels, zest, powders, and even dehydrated wheels all have their uses.

## SHRUBS

Basically sour syrups, shrubs are a great alternative to citrus juice for cramming flavor into a cocktail. Thanks to vinegar, you can customize a shrub with any flavor you can imagine, balance it with a little sugar, and create a bright component to measure up against any spirits in a cocktail. Shrubs keep for a long time if refrigerated in an airtight container.

## SPICES

Bringing the spice cabinet into the mix allows us to tinker with unusual flavor combinations all year long, even when many fresh ingredients are out of season. Most of our recipes call for ground spices, but for the freshest flavor you can source whole spices and grind them with a small spice mill or mortar and pestle.

## SALT

We use fine sea salt to make flavors pop—not to make a drink salty. One way to add a controlled amount of salt to your cocktails is to use a saline solution (page 41), which is easy to make and store behind the bar. Adding only a single drop or two can totally elevate a drink—especially those that have a creamy or chocolatey component. You can also salt the rim of a glass by first wiping the rim with water or fresh citrus juice and then gently rolling only the outer rim (to prevent excess salt from dropping into the drink) against some quality flaky salt.

## WATER AND ICE

From chilling a glass, to chilling and diluting a drink during shaking or stirring, to continuing the chilling and dilution process in the glass once served, cold water and ice are critical cocktail components, ensuring that your first sip is perfect and that the drink stays at the right temperature and texture while you drink it.

Filtered and boiled water will give you the clearest, most solid ice. Appropriately sized cubes that fit your glass not only look great, but also take longer to melt, so it's worth investing in a silicone cocktail ice tray or ice sphere molds if you want to get serious about your drinks.

## SODA

Soda adds a bit of sparkle and, sometimes, a touch of mineral salinity to a cocktail. Just be sure your can or bottle is nice and fresh—and cold!—before topping off a cocktail.

## MILK AND CREAM

Rich and creamy, different plant-based milks can give cocktails a wide range of flavors and textures. We gravitate toward coconut and oat milk, but we've also used soy milk and even lentil-based heavy whipping cream upon occasion. As with all other ingredients, consider what a creamy component is doing in a recipe (adding body? sweetness?) before making a substitution.

## AQUAFABA

Aquafaba, the humble water from a can of chickpeas, has been gaining traction behind cocktail bars as more and more people recognize its near-magical ability to replace egg whites. Vigorous shaking produces amazing white foam to top all your favorite sours and fizzes. It's also great when it comes to baking plant-based meringues (see page 86) and macarons.

# ESSENTIAL BAR TOOLS

From mixing to measuring to filtering, good tools make every step of crafting a cocktail a pleasurable experience. These are the tools we make sure to keep within easy reach behind the bar.

## HARDWARE

**Shakers:** Having several sets of stainless-steel shaker tins on hand for cocktailing is essential. We prefer the dual-tin Boston shaker setups for durability and ease of cleaning, although a cobbler shaker is totally fine if you prefer that style. If you don't have a set of shakers, Mason jars with tight-sealing lids can work in a pinch.

**Mixing Glass:** The glass mixing jars you see on bar tops these days are gorgeous, but they're also expensive and fragile. If you've got one at home collecting dust, we encourage you to put it to use making the recipes in this book. If you don't, any heavy-bottomed vessel, such as a pint glass, will work.

**Barspoon:** A long-handled barspoon is an efficient and nimble choice for stirring. Plus, pouring ingredients over the back of an inverted barspoon when making layered cocktails ensures that the liquid is added gently for distinct layers. If you don't have one, you can get fine results using any long, thin spoon, or even a chopstick or skewer.

For measuring, one barspoon holds 1 teaspoon, or 5 ml, of liquid. A standard set of measuring spoons is always handy for measuring smaller amounts of spirits or spice.

**Muddler:** With a long handle and a wide base, shaped like a mini baseball bat, the muddler allows you to get a good grip and reach the bottom of a shaker or glass to bruise fresh herbs, crush whole spices, or smash fruits to extract their juices and oils.

**Microplane:** Nutmeg, cinnamon sticks, citrus zest—thanks to a microplane, prepping these common garnishes is a breeze.

**Handheld Juicer:** We use a lot of fresh-squeezed citrus juice in our cocktails, and a good handheld press makes our job a lot easier.

## MEASURING

**Jigger:** Jiggers are used to measure small amounts of liquid ingredients. The style you choose is up to you, but make sure you find one with (at least) ¼-, ½-, ¾-, and 1-ounce gradations.

**Scale:** For precision measuring, a kitchen scale is essential for two reasons. First, measuring by weight is far more consistent than measuring by volume. Second, it is much easier to scale a recipe by weight than by volume. For example, if you're having a party for twenty-four people and you are using a recipe that calls for 2 teaspoons or 20 grams of an ingredient, it's simpler to measure 480 grams rather than count all those teaspoons. Boom, sorted. So, please buy a kitchen scale—you won't regret it.

**Pipette:** When recipes call for a few drops (meaning literal droplets), using a pipette allows you to slowly count out an exact amount.

**Bottle Dasher:** These little bottle-topping spouts are perfect for measuring out dashes (a looser term than drops, for when you want to add a very small but not ultraprecise splash) without risk of overpouring.

**Atomizer:** An atomizer is a small bottle capable of spraying a fine mist of liquid. Behind the bar, we sometimes use them to mist the inside of a glass with a small amount of a spirit to add subtle layers of flavor to a drink. If you don't have one, you can achieve a similar effect by rinsing: swirling a small amount of a spirit all around the glass and then discarding the excess.

## FILTERING

**Strainers:** A couple of Hawthorne strainers will make your life much, much easier and a lot less messy when pouring from a shaker or mixing glass into a serving glass. Look for a Hawthorne strainer with a tight spring; the smaller the gaps between the wires, the more sediment the strainer will hold back. Julep strainers have their place but are a little limited in their uses; we don't think they're essential. Small conical fine-mesh strainers are really good for straining out ice chips or small pieces of fruit pulp—anything you don't want in your final product. (Using both a Hawthorne strainer and a conical strainer to produce a perfectly sediment-free drink is known as double-straining.) Larger fine-mesh strainers are handy for filtering syrups or draining liquids from solid ingredients.

**Cheesecloth:** For filtering out tiny particulates that may make it through a fine-mesh strainer, cheesecloth comes in clutch. It also allows you to wring out the maximum amount of liquid from, say, a fruit or nut puree.

**Coffee Filters:** Use a coffee filter for separating even finer gunk like peanut butter or coconut milk solids. If you're feeling spendy, grab a Superbag. They're made of nylon monofilament and are super effective when straining powders or tangles of proteins.

# OUR TAKE ON GLASSWARE

You wouldn't drink beer from a coffee mug, would you? What about champagne from a Solo cup? Glassware greatly impacts how we appreciate our beverages. For reasons both practical (like holding temperature) and sentimental (like personal ritual or family tradition), a drink will often be better received in one vessel over another. Here, we guide you through the glassware we use most frequently. If, after reading, you feel encouraged to expand your personal glassware collection, great! Thrift stores are excellent places to pick up fun cocktail glasses.

And as a rule, all cold cocktails benefit from being served in a chilled glass, especially when they're served neat (with no added ice). Simply place your glasses in the fridge or freezer for a few minutes, or fill them with ice water and let them sit for two minutes before dumping out the water and pouring in the cocktail.

**COUPE** Coupe glasses are wide-mouthed stemmed glasses that look like rounded martini glasses. Great for any cocktail served without ice, the wide mouth allows the drink to open up (interact with air to reveal its nuances) quickly. Coupes are a great fit for sours and fizzes and are sometimes used for serving champagne.

 **COLLINS** A tall tumbler glass, a Collins is best for a higher-volume drink served over ice. Like their skinnier counterpart the highball glass, Collins glasses are a classic fit for easy spirit-mixer drinks like rum and Coke or gin and tonic.

 **ROCKS** The shorter tumbler glass known as a rocks glass is best for serving a spirit neat or with rocks (ice). Some lower-volume cocktails like a Sazerac or Old Fashioned are perfect in a traditional rocks glass. A heavy-bottomed glass is great for muddling and will help keep the drink cold, while thin walls convey elegance.

 **DOUBLE ROCKS** Just a bit larger than a rocks glass, the double rocks can accommodate more voluminous drinks and larger ice cubes or ice spheres.

 **NICK AND NORA** Deeper than a coupe glass and with a softer V-shaped bowl than a martini glass, Nick and Nora glasses are a great stemmed option for any cocktail you wish to serve without ice. Thanks to their smaller diameter and greater height, these glasses will keep drinks cooler for a bit longer than when served in a coupe or martini glass, and may also be easier to carry across the room without spilling!

 **TULIP** This curvy footed glass tapers toward the top. Tulips are great for higher-volume cocktails served on the rocks and when you want to call extra attention to the texture or visuals of the drink, like layers, crushed ice, or a color float.

   **SPECIALTY** Some cocktails require a specific vessel: think a copper cup for a Moscow Mule or a footed glass Irish coffee mug. Most of our recipes rely on standard bar glassware because we prefer to work with sturdy, restaurant-quality brands that we know hold up to frequent use. But when you're at home and can wash everything by hand, it's fun to get creative. Ask your family members for hand-me-downs or visit a thrift store to find some great options that span decades of cocktail culture.

# TECHNIQUES TO KNOW

## SHAKING

Shaking a cocktail chills, dilutes, and emulsifies it all at once. Here's how to do it without making a mess.

* Add your cocktail ingredients to the large tin of a Boston cocktail shaker.

* Add ice to the same tin.

* Invert the small tin over the large tin and get them lined up (the edges should form a straight, almost vertical line along one side).

* Give the top tin a good thump on the bottom to seal the two halves.

* Shake vigorously, using both hands to hold the tins together, starting slow and building into a good rhythm, for 8 to 10 seconds.

To separate the tins, put your thumb on the seam where the tins make the most contact, then squeeze. This should break the seal and allow air into the tins so you can just pop the top off without much resistance.

If you're having trouble separating the tins, give them a smack with the heel of your hand a quarter-turn from that straight vertical line where the tins make the most contact. (If that spot is at 6 o'clock, the smack should be delivered at 3 o'clock with the right hand or 9 o'clock with the left.) Make sure you have a good grip on the tins before delivering this blow!

## DRY SHAKING

When making foamy drinks like sours and fizzes, we prefer to reverse the standard dry-shaking technique, which typically involves shaking a cocktail once without ice to build a foam and then again with ice to chill and dilute it. We've found that shaking with ice first, then again without ice, yields better results when working with plant-based cocktails.

# SHAKING DOS AND DON'TS

 **DO** get comfortable with your shakers. Get a feel for sealing and unsealing them while empty before shaking while filled.

 **DO** vary your grip on the shaker until you find what's most comfortable and stable.

 **DO** vary your shaking motion until you find what's most comfortable for you.

 **DON'T** overfill your shaker. The drink in the shaker needs room to expand. Filling the shaker all the way up may cause it to burst open and leave you covered in cocktail.

 **DON'T** shake a cocktail containing any bubbly or carbonated ingredients. The trapped gas will expand, the pressure will build up, and the shaker may burst open.

## STIRRING

Stirring a drink with ice dilutes the drink without aerating it for a silkier texture than shaken cocktails. Stirring should be a clean, elegant motion, seamlessly pivoting the wrist to keep the ice dancing through the liquid without making too much noise. It may feel awkward at first, but with a small amount of practice, you should be able to stir a drink smoothly.

## STRAINING

Straining your drinks keeps the spent ice and any debris, like citrus pulp or bits of muddled herbs, out of your finished cocktail.

Many drinks will benefit from double-straining through both a Hawthorne strainer and a small conical fine-mesh strainer; the second strainer is meant to catch anything small enough to escape the Hawthorne.

Some drinks don't need to be strained at all and are either built directly in the glass or simply dumped straight from the tin into the glass.

# GARNISHING

When garnishing our drinks, we usually seek either to highlight an existing ingredient, such as by garnishing our Strawberry Smash (page 81) with a fresh strawberry, or to add contrast that makes the drink pop, as with the Tangerine Lace garnish in the Golden Apple (page 146). There are a few basic garnishing techniques that come up time and time again.

**Making Citrus Garnishes:**
Citrus garnishes enliven countless drinks. To make the garnish, first, slice away the ends of the fruit. To make long, uniform strips, run a sharp vegetable peeler over the rind from pole to pole. (The same technique can be used to make long ribbons from other produce, like cucumbers.) To make a citrus twist, use a channel knife to carve out a long, thin strip of zest, then twist into a spiral. To make wedges, cut the citrus in half from pole to pole, then cut lengthwise at an angle to form half-moon shapes. To make wheels, cut thin slices perpendicular to the poles. (You can

use the same technique to make rings or rounds of other produce, like peppers or tomatoes.) Be sure to gently remove any seeds from wheels or wedges. To express a citrus peel, hold the peel gently by the edges, between your thumb and forefinger, skin side toward your drink, and give it a little squeeze. You should see a small spray of oil coat the surface of the drink.

**Making Dehydrated Garnishes:** Several of our drinks call for garnishing with dehydrated citrus wheels. To dehydrate any ingredient, slice it thinly and set the slices in a single layer in a countertop dehydrator until dry and crispy. Alternatively, set the slices on a baking sheet and place on a wire rack in an oven at a very low temperature, monitoring to make sure they don't burn, until dry.

**Making a Mint Cap:** A mint cap is the leafy top of a bunch of mint. To make one, simply break off the longer stems.

**Salting a Rim:** To get salt or other fine ingredients (like spices or sesame seeds) to stick to the rim or side of a glass, first, lightly wet the area with water or another liquid, like citrus juice. Then, while still wet, roll in the salt or press on the desired garnish.

**Stick with Odd Numbers:** The "rule of three" suggests that things are most satisfying in groupings of three. In cocktail land, garnishing with three of a kind doesn't always make sense, but we always try to use an odd number: a single cherry or olive, three berries on a skewer, and so on.

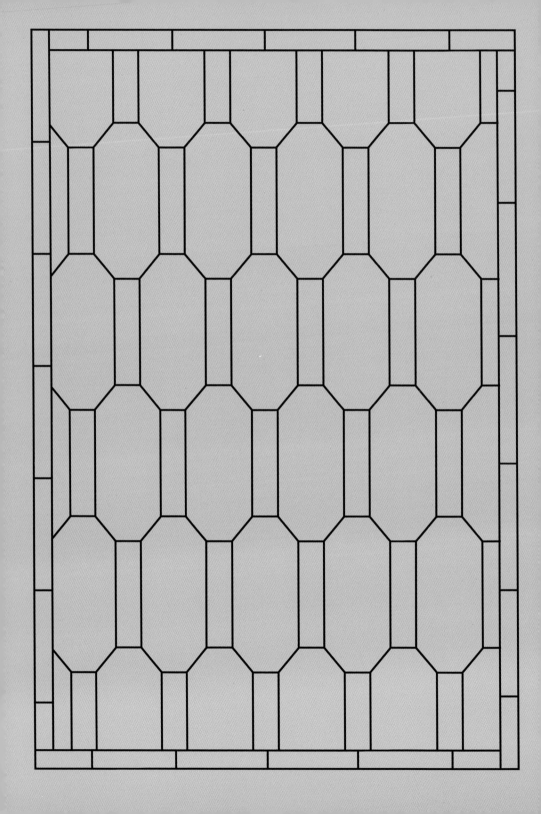

# SPRING

## Drinks

Nothing Sacred 28

Egyptian Limonana 31

Daffodil 34

Rise and Shine 38

Sea Legs 41

Afternoon Snack 42

Bird Leaf 46

Per My Last Email 48

You Can't See Me 52

## Snacks

Hakurei Turnip Brandade 32

Potato Salad with Green Garlic and Pea Shoots 45

White Asparagus with Sauce Gribiche 51

Whipped Black Garlic–Lentil Dip 55

**T**he longer energy is pent up, the more explosive the impact when it's finally released. Whether it's opening a restaurant, launching a new cocktail menu, or perhaps writing a new cocktail cookbook, turning ideas or ingredients into something tangible involves an exhilarating transformation. It's birth, and rebirth. And that's how springtime feels—the transition from winter's stillness and reflection and waiting to a buzzing, magical time full of newfound vitality.

If the seasons can be compared to a dinner party you've been planning for some time, then spring is the moment your friends are finally knocking at the door.

At Vedge, we celebrate this awakening with springtime drinks and snacks that are fresh and green, bright and juicy. Spring veggies are the impatient ones, those that pop up quickly, but are too delicate to hack it through the heat of summer: arugula and lettuces, baby turnips and spicy radishes. Vibrant colors arrive with rainbows of chard and eager beets, and perennials like asparagus shoot up out of the dirt to inspire dishes like our White Asparagus with Sauce Gribiche (page 51). When it comes to the bar, we stick to lighter red wines and rosés, aromatic liquors and frothy, tart sours like the Daffodil (page 34) to wake us up as we embrace the new energy of spring.

If the seasons can be compared to a dinner party you've been planning for some time, then spring is the moment your friends are finally knocking at the door. At Vedge, it's 4:45 PM on a Saturday: Guests are just beginning to arrive, we're shaking our drinks, and the kitchen printer starts clicking away. The party's just getting started, and there's a joyous feast just ahead.

—Kate

# NOTHING SACRED

A terrific garden party aperitif, this cocktail features a New York state specialty: Averell Damson Plum Gin Liqueur. Much like a British sloe gin, it adds a rich texture and soft, rosy hue to this play on a classic daiquiri.—*Brian*

1 ounce (30 ml) Plantation 3 Stars rum

1 ounce (30 ml) dry white wine

0.5 ounce (15 ml) Averell Damson Plum Gin Liqueur

0.5 ounce (15 ml) lemon juice

1 teaspoon Luxardo Maraschino Liqueur

Lemon peel

Chill a Nick and Nora glass.

Add the rum, wine, damson plum gin liqueur, lemon juice, and maraschino liqueur to a cocktail shaker filled with ice and shake for 8 to 10 seconds. Strain into the chilled glass. Express the lemon peel over the drink and use as a garnish.

# EGYPTIAN LIMONANA

Sold at street stands throughout the Nile Valley, this Egyptian lemonade is a blended concoction of fresh mint, whole lemons and limes, and milk. All at once sweet, tart, a touch bitter thanks to the citrus pith, and packed with herbal freshness, this plant-based version made with oat and coconut milk is pretty much the most refreshing thing you can drink.—*Ginevra*

**6 ounces (180 ml) Batched Egyptian Limonana**

**Lime wheel**

**Mint sprig**

Pour the limonana into a Collins glass filled with ice. Garnish with the lime wheel and mint sprig.

## BATCHED EGYPTIAN LIMONANA

Makes about 1 quart (1 L)

**1½ cups (300 g) sugar**

**1 cup (240 ml) oat milk**

**¾ cup plus 1 tablespoon (200 ml) coconut milk**

**¼ cup (15 g) lightly packed mint leaves**

**1 lemon, seeded and chopped**

**½ lime, seeded and chopped**

Combine the sugar, oat milk, and coconut milk, and ¾ cup plus 2 tablespoons (210 ml) water in a blender and blend on high to combine. Add the mint, lemon, and lime, and continue blending just until smooth.

Strain the limonana through a fine-mesh strainer, pressing on the solids with the back of a spoon to extract as much liquid as possible. Store in an airtight container in the fridge for up to 1 day.

 **SPIKE IT**  Try adding 2 ounces (60 ml) of a light Spanish-style rum like Flor de Cana Extra Seco.

# HAKUREI TURNIP BRANDADE

Serves 4 to 6

Turnips come in a wealth of different varieties, and at Vedge, we've had a blast exploring all that we could do with them over the years—from baking them into kimchi cottage pies to sautéing in a creamy Alfredo-style sauce. Hakurei turnips are sweet and quick-growing, one of the first harvests in spring, and they are delightful in our take on brandade, a comforting dip from southern France that just begs to be smeared on some crusty bread.—*Rich*

---

**2 russet potatoes**

**4 cups (520 g) diced Hakurei turnips**

**¼ cup (60 ml) olive oil**

**¼ cup (60 g) minced shallot**

**3 garlic cloves, chopped**

**¼ cup (60 ml) white wine**

**¼ cup (60 g) sauerkraut**

**2 tablespoons capers, drained**

**2 tablespoons nutritional yeast**

**2 teaspoons salt**

**2 teaspoons pepper**

**1 cup (220 g) vegan mayonnaise**

**⅓ cup (75 g) vegan butter**

**Baguette slices**

Preheat the oven to 450°F (230°C). Wrap the potatoes in foil and bake for about 45 minutes, just until tender. Remove from the oven and let cool.

Reduce the heat to 400°F (200°C).

Coat the turnips in half the olive oil and roast on a baking sheet until tender, about 10 minutes.

Sauté the shallot and garlic in the remaining olive oil in a small saucepan over medium heat until browned, about 3 minutes, then deglaze the pan with the wine. Add the sauerkraut, capers, nutritional yeast, salt, and pepper to the pan and cook for 2 minutes. Add ½ cup (120 ml) water and bring to a boil, then reduce the heat to low and simmer for 10 minutes.

Once the potatoes are cool enough to handle, carefully remove their skins. Rice them over a medium bowl using a box grater or ricer. Add the mayonnaise and butter, the contents of the saucepan, and the roasted turnips. Gently mix, then let rest for 10 minutes to allow the flavors to meld.

In small batches, pulse the mixture in a food processor for a few seconds at a time, just until the turnips have broken down. The texture should be creamy with lots of fine shreds of roasted turnip.

Transfer the mixture to a casserole dish or divide it between 6 individual ramekins. Warm it in the 400°F (200°C) oven for about 10 minutes, just until the top begins to brown. Serve with the baguette slices.

**PAIR WITH . . . Rise and Shine** (page 38); the wine offers a clean-tasting contrast to this decadent bar snack.

# DAFFODIL

Early spring is rough in the Northeast and Mid-Atlantic as we wait for the slush to melt and the season's first produce to mature. Blooming daffodils are usually our first sign that winter has begun to lose its grip. Inspired by those intrepid flowers, and a nod to the beloved cake recipe by the same name, this cheery cocktail is just the drink for welcoming spring. It's worth going to the extra effort to make the Quick Mint; the garnish is both herbaceous and slightly tart and offers a counterpoint to the sweet and creamy cocktail.—*Kate*

| | |
|---|---|
| 0.5 ounce (15 ml) Quick Mint | 0.5 ounce (15 ml) Saffron Syrup |
| 1 ounce (30 ml) Cocchi Americano | 1.5 ounces (45 ml) Beefeater gin |
| 0.5 ounce (15 ml) aquafaba | 1 ounce (30 ml) plain vegan yogurt |
| 0.5 ounce (15 ml) lemon juice | Mint sprig |

Pour the Quick Mint into a tulip glass, then fill the glass with ice.

Add the Cocchi Americano, aquafaba, lemon juice, and syrup to a cocktail shaker, fill the shaker with ice, and shake vigorously for 8 to 10 seconds to generate a foam. Carefully strain into the glass over the back of a barspoon to form a second layer. Discard the ice.

Add the gin and yogurt to the shaker, fill it with fresh ice, and shake for 8 to 10 seconds to chill. Strain, discard the ice, return the mixture to the shaker, and dry shake for 8 to 10 seconds to emulsify. Carefully pour into the glass over the back of a barspoon to form a third layer. Garnish with the mint sprig.

## SAFFRON SYRUP

Makes about 1 cup (240 ml)

½ cup (100 g) sugar

1 lemon, seeded and thinly sliced

½ teaspoon saffron

Combine the sugar, lemon, and saffron with 1 cup (240 ml) water in a medium saucepan over medium heat. Heat until the water starts to boil, then reduce the heat to low and simmer until the lemon slices are translucent, about 5 minutes.

Carefully transfer the syrup to a blender. Blend until smooth, then strain, discarding the solids. Let the syrup cool completely, then store it in an airtight container in the fridge for up to 1 week.

# QUICK MINT

Makes about 1 cup (240 ml)

**½ cup (100 g) sugar**

**⅛ teaspoon agar powder**

**1 lime, zested and juiced**

**¼ cup (15 g) lightly packed mint leaves**

Combine the sugar and agar powder with 1 cup (240 ml) water in a small saucepan over medium heat and bring to a simmer. Cook until the mixture has reduced by half, about 10 minutes.

Let the mixture cool completely, then transfer it to a blender. Add the lime zest, lime juice, and mint, and blend on low speed until all the mint leaves have broken down.

Strain the mixture through a fine-mesh strainer, discarding the solids. Store it in an airtight container in the fridge for up to 3 days.

*Daffodil*

# RISE AND SHINE

In this drink, humble root vegetables—either from your cellar or pulled right out of the dirt in early spring—flaunt their sweet, earthy spice against the bitter tones found in orange wine and a nutty, oxidized French-style rancio. With a boost of salt from the garnish, this is a drink that fires on all cylinders! Any orange wine will do as a base, though a racy Georgian wine with apricot notes and chewy tannins will work best. If you can't get your hands on a rancio, substitute a dry sherry.—*Kate*

| | |
|---|---|
| 0.5 ounce (15 ml) lemon juice | 1 ounce (30 ml) rancio |
| Coarse black salt | 1 ounce (30 ml) Golden Root Syrup |
| 1.5 ounces (45 ml) orange wine | 1 ounce (30 ml) soda water |

Chill a Collins glass, then then brush the side of the glass lightly with some of the lemon juice, roll the outer rim in the salt, and fill the glass with ice.

Add the orange wine, rancio, syrup, and remaining lemon juice to a cocktail shaker. Fill the shaker with ice and shake for 8 to 10 seconds. Strain the cocktail into the prepared glass and top with the soda water.

## GOLDEN ROOT SYRUP

Makes about 1½ cups (360 ml)

½ cup (120 ml) agave syrup

1 large or 2 medium golden beets, peeled and chopped

1-inch (2.5 cm) piece fresh turmeric, peeled and chopped

1-inch (2.5 cm) piece fresh ginger, peeled and chopped

Combine the agave syrup, beets, turmeric, and ginger with 1 cup (240 ml) water in a medium saucepan and heat over high heat until the mixture comes to a boil.

Reduce the heat to low and simmer until the beets are tender, about 10 minutes.

Let the mixture cool completely, then strain through a fine-mesh strainer (ideally lined with cheesecloth), pressing on the solids with the back of a spoon to extract as much liquid as possible. Discard the solids. Store the syrup in an airtight container in the fridge for up to 1 week.

# SEA LEGS

Originally inspired by a cocktail made with sugar snap peas from The Clover Club in New York, this drink took many twists and turns before ending up as it is. The name comes from the line "I got my sea legs" in the Run the Jewels song. Vivid green, this cocktail is an eye-catcher, but beneath the surface it's laced with unexpected smoky, earthy flavor. It's also fresh and bright made with gin instead of mezcal, if you feel like switching things up.—*Brian and Ginevra*

1.5 ounces (45 ml) Banhez mezcal

0.75 ounce (22 ml) lemon juice

0.75 ounce (22 ml) Sugar Snap Pea Syrup

0.5 ounce (15 ml) Salers gentian

3 drops orange blossom water

3 drops Saline Solution

Nasturtium or pansy, optional

Chill a coupe glass.

Combine the mezcal, lemon juice, syrup, gentian, orange blossom water, and saline in a cocktail shaker. Fill the shaker with ice and shake for 8 to 10 seconds, then strain through a Hawthorne strainer held over a conical strainer into the chilled glass. Garnish with the nasturtium, if using.

## SUGAR SNAP PEA SYRUP

Makes about 1 cup (240 ml)

**2 cups (160 g) sugar snap peas**

**1 cup (200 g) sugar**

**¼ teaspoon citric acid or lemon juice**

Juice the peas using a vegetable juicer. Alternatively, roughly chop the peas and add them to a blender with just enough water to engage the blades, about ¼ cup (60 ml), blend, and then strain the juice through a fine-mesh strainer.

Add the juice, sugar, and citric acid to a blender and blend on low just until the sugar dissolves. Store the syrup in an airtight container in the fridge for up to 2 days.

## SALINE SOLUTION

Makes about ¼ cup (60 ml)

**1 tablespoon plus 1 teaspoon salt**

Combine the salt with ¼ cup (60 ml) water in a bowl and stir until the salt is dissolved.

Store in an airtight container for up to 6 weeks.

# AFTERNOON SNACK

Them: Don't play with your food.

Us: Get bent. We'll play with our food if we want.

This Old Fashioned–style drink with celery and peanut butter never fails to put us in a playful mood, reminding us of that favorite childhood snack, ants on a log, enjoyed after a rainy spring morning spent jumping in puddles. If you're feeling especially nostalgic, you can serve it with a peanut butter–smeared celery stick dotted with a few sherry-soaked raisins for a grown-up take on the classic snack.—*Brian*

**1.5 ounces (45 g) Peanut Butter–Washed Bourbon**

**0.5 ounce (15 ml) Pedro Ximénez sherry**

**0.5 ounce (15 ml) Celery Syrup**

**2 dashes celery bitters**

**1 dash orange bitters**

**Small celery slice**

**3 raisins**

Place a large ice cube into a double rocks glass. Add the bourbon, sherry, syrup, and bitters to the glass and stir until chilled, 8 to 10 seconds. Thread the celery slice and raisins onto a skewer and use as a garnish.

## PEANUT BUTTER–WASHED BOURBON

Makes about 1½ cups (360 ml)

**1½ cups (360 ml) Wild Turkey 101 bourbon**

**1 tablespoon creamy peanut butter**

Add the bourbon and peanut butter to a bowl and whisk until well combined, about 2 minutes. Store the mixture in an airtight container for at least 12 hours, ideally overnight, to allow the flavors to meld.

Strain the mixture through a fine-mesh strainer lined with a coffee filter, repeating the straining as necessary until perfectly clear. (Be patient; resist pushing the mixture through the strainer, or the bourbon will be muddy.) The bourbon will keep in an airtight container in the fridge for at least 1 week.

# CELERY SYRUP

Makes about 1 cup (240 ml)

**1½ cups (180 g) chopped celery**
**¾ cup plus 1 tablespoon (160 g) sugar**
**⅛ teaspoon citric acid or lemon juice**

Juice the celery using a vegetable juicer. (If you don't have a juicer, finely chop the celery and add it to a blender with just enough water to engage the blades, about ¼ cup (60 ml), then strain the juice through a fine-mesh strainer.)

Combine the celery juice, sugar, and citric acid in a blender and blend on low until the sugar dissolves. Blending on low speed prevents the mixture from heating up so the green color stays vibrant. The syrup can be stored in an airtight container in the fridge for 2 to 3 days.

# POTATO SALAD
## with Green Garlic and Pea Shoots

Serves 2 to 4

I get antsy in early spring. There are little green shoots all over the garden, but nothing is quite ready . . . but soon! This dish is a celebration of some of the first gifts of the new year from our home garden, Lost Glove: pea shoots and green garlic or garlic scapes.—*Rich*

---

**4 Yukon Gold or other waxy potatoes, cut into 1-inch (2.5 cm) cubes**

**1 teaspoon salt**

**1 tablespoon plus ½ cup (135 ml) olive oil**

**½ cup (75 g) chopped green garlic**

**1 cup (85 g) pea shoots, chopped**

**½ cup (110 g) vegan mayonnaise**

**¼ cup (30 g) capers, drained**

**¼ cup (15 g) lightly packed parsley**

**¼ cup (40 g) chopped red onion**

**¼ cup (25 g) chopped scallions (white part only)**

**2 tablespoons chopped fresh dill**

**2 tablespoons lemon juice**

**1 tablespoon lemon zest**

**1 teaspoon pepper**

Fill a large pot with water and add the potatoes and salt. Bring to a boil over high heat and cook just until the potatoes are tender, 8 to 12 minutes, then drain the potatoes and place them on a baking sheet to cool.

Heat 1 tablespoon of the oil in a small saucepan over medium heat. Add the green garlic and sauté for 3 minutes, then remove the pan from the heat and allow the garlic to cool.

Combine the pea shoots, mayonnaise, capers, parsley, onion, scallions, dill, lemon juice and zest, and pepper with the garlic, the remaining oil, and ¼ cup (60 ml) water in a food processor and pulse until the vegetables are mostly broken down, with some texture remaining.

Pour the dressing over the cooled potatoes and toss to coat. Chill for at least 2 hours before serving.

 **PAIR WITH . . . Sea Legs** (page 41) to lean into an all-green color scheme.

# BIRD LEAF

We can get a little impatient while waiting to harvest the first of the spring produce. When we find ourselves craving bright flavors in early spring, our stash of citrus marmalade comes to the rescue. Sipping on this cocktail, made with bergamot marmalade, floral vermouth, gentian, and elderflower, is an act of wishful thinking and hope for brighter days. Marmalade made with fresh bergamot is key to the drink's character, and there's no real substitute for its flavor, but if you can't find it, you can use another multi-dimensional citrus like grapefruit or Meyer lemon for a unique take on this cocktail.—*Brian*

1.5 ounces (45 ml) Dolin Dry vermouth

0.5 ounce (15 ml) Salers gentian

0.5 ounce (15 ml) Luksusowa Vodka

0.25 ounce (7 ml) St. Germain elderflower liqueur

1 teaspoon Bergamot Marmalade

Bergamot or orange peel

Chill a coupe glass.

Add the vermouth, gentian, vodka, liqueur, and marmalade to a mixing glass filled with ice and stir until well chilled. Strain through a Hawthorne strainer held over a conical strainer into the chilled glass. Garnish with the bergamot peel.

## BERGAMOT MARMALADE
### Makes about 1 cup (320 g)

2 medium bergamots

1 tablespoon lemon juice

1 cup (200 g) sugar

1 teaspoon agave syrup

Zest the bergamots, then peel. Working over a bowl to catch any juice, carefully separate the citrus into segments using a paring knife. Add the bergamot zest and segments and the lemon juice to the bowl with the collected bergamot juice. Reserve the zested peel, pith, and core in a second bowl. Add ½ cup (120 ml) water to each bowl, then cover both bowls and store them in the fridge for at least 6 hours or ideally overnight.

Add the peel mixture to a medium saucepan and simmer over low heat for 30 minutes or until the peels have become translucent. Strain the mixture through a fine-mesh strainer lined with cheesecloth and press on the solids using the back of a spoon to extract as much liquid as possible. Discard the solids. (This pectin-rich liquid will be sticky!)

Next, add the bergamot segment mixture to a medium saucepan with the strained pectin liquid and simmer over low heat for about 10 minutes, until the liquid is reduced by half.

Add the sugar and continue simmering on low, stirring occasionally, for another 5 minutes or until the sugar is completely dissolved and the liquid has just started to boil. Test the consistency by scooping some of the marmalade up with a spoon and holding it away from the heat. If the marmalade tightens on the cold spoon, it's ready. If it runs off, simmer the mixture for another 2 to 4 minutes, then test again.

Add the agave syrup, stir, then remove the saucepan from the heat. Allow the marmalade to cool completely before storing it in an airtight container in the fridge for up to 1 month.

# PER MY LAST EMAIL

Round about mid-March, we find ourselves wishing we were lounging on a beach somewhere—anywhere! In lieu of that, we turn to the warmer parts of the world for cocktail inspiration. Amchur powder (made from dried, unripe mango) and lime make a bright cordial that plays nicely with the funky-sweet flavor of papaya in this playful take on a daiquiri. To save work, we like to use a lightly sweetened store-bought papaya puree like Les Vergers Boiron. Now, close the laptop: You're on vacation—at least until the glass is empty.—*Brian*

1.5 ounces (45 ml) Plantation 3 Stars rum

0.75 ounce (22 ml) lime juice

0.75 ounce (22 ml) papaya puree

0.5 ounce (15 ml) Gosling's Black Seal rum

0.5 ounce (15 ml) Lime-Amchur Cordial

1 teaspoon Smith & Cross rum

Pinch of salt

Dehydrated lime wheel

Add the Plantation rum, lime juice, papaya, Gosling's rum, cordial, Smith & Cross rum, and salt to a cocktail shaker. Fill the shaker with ice and shake for 8 to 10 seconds. Strain into a rocks glass filled with ice. Garnish with the dehydrated lime wheel.

## LIME-AMCHUR CORDIAL

Makes about ½ cup (120 ml)

3 limes

¾ cup (150 g) sugar

1 teaspoon amchur powder

Peel the limes using a vegetable peeler. Add the lime peels, sugar, and amchur powder to a bowl and muddle.

Cover and let the mixture rest at room temperature for at least 6 hours or ideally overnight to allow the flavors to meld.

Transfer the mixture to a medium saucepan with ½ cup (120 ml) water, and cook over medium-low heat, stirring occasionally, until the sugar dissolves, 4 to 5 minutes.

Allow the mixture to cool completely, then strain using a fine-mesh strainer, discarding the solids. Store the syrup in an airtight container in the fridge for up to 1 week.

# WHITE ASPARAGUS
## with Sauce Gribiche

*Serves 2*

Maybe I'm just a culinary romantic, but in spring all I want to do is sit at a café table in a small French village, drinking wine and eating the classics. Or better yet, a patio among the olive tree groves and lavender fields, with good friends and great conversation. This idyllic daydream has inspired many a dish in my career, including this one. Gribiche, one of the lesser-known French sauces, is basically a mayonnaise studded with capers, cornichons, and hard-boiled egg, green with spring herbs and gently spiced with Dijon mustard. Here, I've simply substituted tofu for the egg. If good white asparagus is unavailable, then green is just fine.—*Rich*

---

**½ cup (110 g) vegan mayonnaise**

**1 tablespoon lightly packed parsley**

**1 tablespoon lightly packed tarragon leaves**

**1 tablespoon minced shallot**

**1 tablespoon olive oil**

**2 teaspoons Dijon mustard**

**½ teaspoon pepper**

**¼ teaspoon salt**

**1 tablespoon chopped cornichons**

**1 tablespoon capers, drained**

**3 ounces (85 g) smoked firm tofu, cut into ¼-inch (6 mm) cubes**

**0.5 pound (225 g) white asparagus**

**1 tablespoon vegetable oil**

Combine the mayonnaise, parsley, tarragon, shallot, oil, mustard, pepper, and salt in a food processor. Pulse until smooth, about 1 minute. Add the cornichons and capers and pulse 3 times to incorporate.

Transfer the mixture to a bowl, and fold in the tofu, then set aside.

Cut off and discard the tough bottom third of the asparagus spears, then slice them on the bias into 1-inch (2.5 cm) pieces.

Heat the oil in a large skillet over medium heat and then sear the asparagus pieces until they start to brown on the edges, about 2 minutes. Remove from the pan to retain a crunchy texture.

Toss the asparagus with the sauce, and serve.

**PAIR WITH . . . You Can't See Me** (page 52) for a partner of equally bold standing, grassy and fragrant with Chareau and chamomile.

# YOU CAN'T SEE ME

This drink's name comes from a silly private joke between me and my fellow Vedge bartenders. After prepping the chamomile-infused rye, we labeled the bottle "CAMO" as shorthand—and from there, it didn't take us long to start joking that we could no longer see it. Infusing spirits is a simple technique, but one that can instantly add dimension to your cocktail game. Using dried chamomile flowers in the rye infusion makes it possible to serve this cocktail year-round, but in spring, when chamomile is in season, we like to garnish it with the fresh flowers.—*Brian*

**1.5 ounces (45 ml) Chamomile-Infused Rye**

**0.5 ounce (15 ml) Chareau**

**0.5 ounce (15 ml) Simple Syrup (page 10)**

**0.25 ounce (7 ml) Rittenhouse Rye**

**6 drops preserved lemon brine**

**2 dashes Angostura bitters**

**Mint cap or fresh chamomile flowers**

Chill a Nick and Nora glass.

Add the chamomile rye, Chareau, syrup, Rittenhouse Rye, brine, and bitters to a mixing glass filled with ice and stir until chilled, 8 to 10 seconds. Strain into the chilled glass. Garnish with the mint cap.

## CHAMOMILE-INFUSED RYE

Makes about 1½ cups (360 ml)

**1½ cups (360 ml) George Dickel Rye**

**1 tablespoon dried chamomile flowers**

Combine the rye and chamomile in a small bowl, cover, and let rest for 2 hours. Strain the mixture through a fine-mesh strainer and discard the solids. Store in an airtight container in the fridge for up to 2 weeks.

# WHIPPED BLACK GARLIC–LENTIL DIP

Serves 4 to 6

Every cocktail party needs a good dip, and this one—our reinvented version of a classic onion dip, enriched with lentils for extra body—is always a massive hit. Black garlic is the result of a long aging process that turns fresh garlic soft and rich, with a little umami funk, like candied onions. There's no real substitute for that flavor, but if you can't find it you can try making this recipe with roasted garlic. If you can't find Montreal Steak Seasoning, you can approximate it with equal parts kosher salt, pepper, paprika, garlic powder, onion powder, coriander, dill, and cayenne. For extra indulgence, add a bit of truffle puree. Serve with crackers or crudites.—*Rich*

1 cup (260 g) canned black lentils, drained

1 cup (55 g) crispy onions

½ cup (120 g) vegan cream cheese

½ cup (120 g) vegan sour cream

½ cup (110 g) vegan mayonnaise

12 black garlic cloves

1 tablespoon Dijon mustard

1 teaspoon Montreal Steak Seasoning (see headnote)

½ teaspoon salt

½ teaspoon pepper

Combine the lentils, onions, cream cheese, sour cream, mayonnaise, black garlic, mustard, steak seasoning, salt, and pepper with ¼ cup (60 ml) water in a food processor and process until smooth and creamy, about 2 minutes.

 **PAIR WITH . . . Per My Last Email** (page 48). The tangy black garlic does magical things with the fruity papaya.

# EARLY SUMMER

## Drinks

## Snacks

We like the unexpected in our cocktails. It's safe to say that most of our fellow bartenders feel the same way. Watching a guest's face when they take those first few sips of a new cocktail makes us glow with pride. Seeing people pass a drink to their dining companions with a "You've gotta try this" is our driving force.

When developing new cocktails, usually the season and our standing drink menu lineup provide our starting point. In the summer, that generally means looking to refreshing flavors, drinks bursting with juicy summer fruit like Even Cowgirls Get the Blues (page 94) or Strawberry Smash (page 81). But balance is important, in menus and in individual drinks. It's good to keep some spirit-forward drinks on the menu so everyone can find something they like—a little bitterness to counter the sweet. Sometimes that bitter element adds just the right amount of dynamic tension to transform a drink from flat or "flabby" to a beverage in which every ingredient shines.

The fine-tuning can be an agonizing process. Now that we've got the right balance and combination of flavors, how do we present it? What

Naming a thing gives it power, permanence, a reference point in the world.

glass should it go in? What's the garnish? Does it get ice? Big ice or small? How does it taste when it's been sitting for twenty minutes?

After all that decision-making, it's the naming that's the hardest part. Naming a thing gives it power, permanence, a reference point in the world. The name is often the most personal part of cocktail creation for us, as we pull names from our lived experience, our favorite media, our conversations. Sometimes our drink names are directly referential, as in Mr. Frond (page 78). Other times they take the long way round, as in the Headbanger (page 181). In either case, the naming is what sets a drink free—out of our hands at last, and into yours.

—Brian

# DON'T CALL ME SHIRLEY

When the Beverage Media declares a drink "on-trend," sometimes you just have to fall in line. Our version of the Dirty Shirley—a vodka-spiked Shirley Temple and 2022's drink of the summer—goes hard, with a bright-red syrup made from fresh, tart cherries. The name, a joke from the movie *Airplane*, was a no-brainer.—*Brian*

| | |
|---|---|
| 1 lime wheel | 0.75 ounce (22 ml) Tart Cherry Syrup |
| 1 cocktail cherry | 0.5 ounce (15 ml) lime juice |
| 2 ounces (60 ml) Luksusowa Vodka | 3 ounces (90 ml) soda water |

Skewer one edge of the lime wheel with a toothpick, then skewer the cherry. Fold the lime wheel halfway around the cherry and then skewer the opposite edge to hold it in place. Set the cherry flag aside for garnishing.

Add the vodka, syrup, and lime juice to a Collins glass. Top with the soda water, fill the glass with ice, and stir until chilled, 8 to 10 seconds. Garnish with the cherry flag.

## TART CHERRY SYRUP

Makes about 1 cup (240 ml)

**1 cup (150 g) fresh tart cherries, pitted**

**¾ cup (150 g) sugar**

Combine the cherries and sugar in a bowl, stir to coat, and then cover and refrigerate for at least 6 hours or ideally overnight.

Add ½ cup (120 ml) water to the cherry mixture and stir until the sugar dissolves.

Strain through a fine-mesh strainer. Reserve the cherries for another use (they're delicious on ice cream!) and store the syrup in an airtight container in the fridge for up to 1 week.

**UN-SPIKE IT** Omit the vodka to turn this drink into a refreshing nonalcoholic soda.

# FRONT PORCH SWING

A Manhattan is big, crowded, and loud—just like its island namesake. Inspired by the classic drink, our Front Porch Swing takes that big-city complexity out to the hills for a bit of R&R. Slow it down. Set a spell. Mix yourself a pitcher to sip in the early evening as the fireflies are just starting to come out. You'll soon see why city life isn't all it's cracked up to be.—*Brian*

**3 ounces (90 ml) Batched Front Porch Swing**

**Lemon peel twist**

Chill a Nick and Nora glass.

Pour the cocktail into the chilled glass and garnish with the lemon twist.

## BATCHED FRONT PORCH SWING

Makes about 4 cups (1 L)

**1½ cups (360 ml) Powers Irish Whiskey**

**¾ cup (180 ml) Cocchi Americano**

**½ cup (120 ml) Rothman & Winter Apricot Liqueur**

**½ cup (120 ml) Amontillado sherry**

Combine the whiskey, Cocchi Americano, liqueur, sherry, and ½ cup plus 2 tablespoons (150 ml) water in a large bowl. Transfer the mixture to an airtight container and freeze for at least 3 hours or ideally overnight. The cocktail can be stored in the freezer for up to 6 months.

# MRS. DOUBTFIRE

The Old Fashioned is many things—bold, brash, and more complex than it seems at first taste. But in its familiarity, it can sometimes come across as a bit too predictable. This variation shows that the classic formula can be delicate, floral, and a helluva lot of fun.—*Brian*

**1.75 ounces (50 ml) Famous Grouse Blended Scotch**

**0.75 ounce (22 ml) Rhubarb-Lavender Shrub**

**0.75 ounce (7 ml) Amaro Montenegro**

**4 dashes Peychaud's bitters**

**Lemon peel**

**Fresh lavender sprig**

Add the Scotch, shrub, amaro, and bitters to a mixing glass. Fill the glass with ice and stir until chilled, 8 to 10 seconds, then strain into a double rocks glass with one big ice cube. Express the lemon peel over the drink, then garnish with the lemon peel and the lavender sprig.

## RHUBARB-LAVENDER SHRUB

Makes about 1 cup (240 ml)

**1 large stalk fresh rhubarb, chopped**

**½ cup (100 g) sugar**

**1 teaspoon chopped fresh lavender**

**2 teaspoons champagne vinegar**

Heat the rhubarb, sugar, and ¼ cup plus 3 tablespoons (100 ml) water in a medium saucepan over low heat, stirring often, until the sugar has dissolved and the rhubarb has softened, about 10 minutes. Remove from the heat, add the lavender, and steep for 10 minutes.

Strain the mixture through a fine-mesh strainer, discarding the solids. Add the vinegar and let the syrup cool completely. The syrup will keep in an airtight container in the fridge for at least 1 week.

# SUMMER SQUASH
## with Avocado and Aguachile

*Serves 4*

Our chef Elpidio and his right hand, Bernie, have been part of the Vedge kitchen since we opened our doors in 2011. A few years ago, El introduced us to aguachile, a gazpacho-like sauce made with cucumbers, cilantro, lime juice, and green chiles, and we were blown away by both its freshness and simplicity. When you first taste it, you'll want to drink it by the cup! We've paired it here with some quick-roasted summer squash and smashed avocado, but it goes well with almost any grilled vegetable and can even be served on its own as an alternative to gazpacho.—*Rich*

---

**4 cups (450 g) zucchini or summer squash noodles**

**3½ teaspoons salt**

**2 cucumbers, chopped**

**¾ cup (45 g) lightly packed cilantro, chopped**

**1 tablespoon lime juice**

**1 tablespoon chopped, seeded jalapeño**

**1 garlic clove, chopped**

**½ teaspoon pepper**

**3 tablespoons olive oil**

**½ teaspoon chipotle chile powder**

**2 teaspoons ground cumin**

**½ cup (120 g) chopped tomato**

**¼ cup (60 g) chopped red onion**

**2 avocados**

Toss the zucchini noodles in a colander set over a bowl with 2 teaspoons of the salt. Let the noodles sit for about 30 minutes, until they've released their excess liquid. While the noodles sit, preheat the oven to 400°F (200°C).

To make the aguachile, add the cucumbers, ¼ cup (15 g) of the cilantro, the lime juice, jalapeño, garlic, pepper, 1 teaspoon of the salt, and ½ cup (120 ml) water to a blender and blend until smooth, about 1 minute.

Toss the noodles with 2 tablespoons of the oil and the chipotle and cumin, then spread on a baking sheet and roast until the noodles begin to turn golden brown, about 5 minutes.

Remove the noodles from the oven and let cool completely, about 10 minutes, before tossing with the tomato, onion, and remaining cilantro.

Using a fork, smash the avocados with the remaining 1 tablespoon of olive oil and ½ teaspoon of salt.

In the center of a dinner plate, add one quarter of the smashed avocado to a ring mold and gently unmold to form a pedestal. Twist one quarter of the noodles into a bundle atop the avocado and surround with some of the aguachile. Repeat three more times with the remaining ingredients on the other plates, and serve.

**PAIR WITH . . . Sharkskin Suit** (page 70). Equal parts spicy and refreshing, the aguachile's herbal salinity is sensational with the sweet melon.

# MOROCCAN FRUIT PUNCH

This is my re-creation of a drink that I first enjoyed at a small traditional restaurant in the heart of Tangier. Morocco is a Muslim country in which alcohol is mostly provided for tourists, so this was an unexpected nonalcoholic delight, a complimentary sweet drink that they kept refilling. I asked what was in it and they said it was a secret recipe—but I've done my best to approximate its syrupy character. Its sweetness makes it a beautiful pairing for something spicy and bright.—*Ginevra*

**6 ounces Batched Moroccan Fruit Punch**

**Pomegranate seeds**

Pour the punch into a Moroccan tea glass or a Collins glass filled with ice and garnish with the pomegranate seeds.

## BATCHED MOROCCAN FRUIT PUNCH

Makes about 2 cups (480 ml)

**1½ cups (360 ml) prune juice**

**½ cup (120 ml) pomegranate juice**

**1 tablespoon date syrup**

Add the prune juice, pomegranate juice, and date syrup to a bowl and whisk to combine. Pour the mixture into a large pitcher, fill the pitcher with ice, and stir until chilled, 8 to 10 seconds. Serve immediately.

# SHARKSKIN SUIT

Just like its namesake, this elegant martini is set apart by its smooth, satiny texture—perfect for both keeping you cool on hot summer nights and wowing a crowd. Clarifying the cantaloupe juice requires a little finesse (we highly recommend using a kitchen scale and thermometer), but it's worth the effort.—*Brian*

1.5 ounces (45 ml) Turmeric-Ginger Vodka

1 ounce (30 ml) Clarified Cantaloupe Juice

0.75 ounce (22 ml) Dolin Blanc vermouth

½ cantaloupe ball, skewered

Chill a Nick and Nora glass.

Add the vodka, cantaloupe juice, and vermouth to a mixing glass. Fill the glass with ice and stir until chilled, 8 to 10 seconds, then strain into the chilled glass. Garnish with the halved cantaloupe ball.

## TURMERIC-GINGER VODKA

Makes about 1½ cups (360 ml)

1½ cups (360 ml) Boyd & Blair Potato Vodka

1-inch (1.25 cm) piece turmeric, thinly sliced

1-inch (1.25 cm) piece ginger, thinly sliced

Combine vodka, turmeric, and ginger in a bowl, cover, and let rest for at least 8 hours, ideally overnight. Strain using a fine-mesh strainer, discarding the solids. Store the vodka in an airtight container for up to 2 weeks.

# CLARIFIED CANTALOUPE JUICE

Makes 1¾ cups (360 ml)

**4½ cups (700 g) cubed cantaloupe**

**1 teaspoon agar powder**

Combine the cantaloupe and ¼ cup (60 ml) water in a blender and blend on low until liquefied, about 1 minute. Cover and let sit at room temperature for 1 to 2 hours.

Add 1 cup (240 ml) water to a medium saucepan with the agar powder and bring to boil over medium heat, stirring constantly. Reduce the heat to low and simmer for 5 minutes.

Very slowly, stream in the juice, stirring constantly to ensure even distribution. Use a thermometer to ensure that the temperature of the mixture doesn't drop below 95°F (35°C). (If you add too much juice at once and drop the temperature, the agar will solidify prematurely.)

Once the juice is fully incorporated, remove from the heat and let cool before transferring to an airtight container and freezing overnight.

Later, invert the frozen mixture into a fine-mesh strainer set over a large bowl to collect the clarified juice as the mixture thaws, about 2 hours. Do not press on the mixture as it thaws—you want the fibers in the cantaloupe left behind with the agar proteins, capturing clear, aromatic juice.

Once the mixture has fully thawed and drained, discard the solids and store the juice in an airtight container in the fridge for up to 4 days.

*Sharkskin Suit*

# WHITE BEAN TAGINE

*Serves 4 to 6*

Amid the abundance of a Moroccan dinner table, with its feast of vegetable side dishes, the tagine has a commanding presence, with its spice-laced, heady fragrance billowing from its namesake cooking vessel's volcano-like cone. This riff on the original is a great small plate for a cocktail party, ideally served from its namesake earthenware cooking pot or individual warm ramekins. It can also be a full meal when paired with couscous and baked vegetables. A small dish of green olives sprinkled with lemon zest makes a great accompaniment.—*Rich*

---

**¼ cup (60 ml) olive oil**

**¼ cup (40 g) chopped onion**

**2 garlic cloves, minced**

**2 tomatoes, roughly chopped**

**1 tablespoon ras el hanout**

**1 teaspoon salt**

**1 teaspoon pepper**

**1½ cups (360 ml) vegetable stock**

**2 cups (520 g) canned cannellini beans or chickpeas**

**¼ cup (55 g) vegan butter**

**¼ cup (15 g) lightly packed cilantro, chopped**

**1 tablespoon lemon juice**

Heat the oil in a large pot over medium heat. Add the onion and cook until golden brown, about 3 minutes, then add the garlic and cook for another 30 seconds, until fragrant. Add the tomatoes, ras el hanout, salt, and pepper and continue to cook until the tomatoes start to break down and form a paste, about 5 minutes.

Add the stock, reduce the heat to low, and simmer until the vegetables have softened, about 12 minutes. Add the beans and simmer for another 5 minutes, until heated through.

Remove from the heat and stir in the butter, cilantro, and lemon juice. Serve immediately.

---

 **PAIR WITH ...** **Moroccan Fruit Punch** (page 69) to transport yourself to Morocco without having to jump on a plane.

# PRINCETON CLUB

Vedge opened in 2011 in the historic Princeton Club of Philadelphia, also known as the Tiger Building. Princeton Club is also the perfect name for this riff on the pre-Prohibition-era Clover Club, another drink that originated in Philadelphia. Our adaptation uses tart wineberries—a wild fruit that peaks locally in early summer—but you can easily substitute other sour fruits like rhubarb in late spring or cranberry in the fall. Alternatively, you can halve the amount of sugar in the syrup and use a sweeter berry like raspberry or blueberry.—*Kate*

| | |
|---|---|
| 3 fresh wineberries | 0.75 ounce (22 ml) aquafaba |
| 1.5 ounces (45 ml) Bluecoat American Dry Gin | 0.75 ounce (22 ml) lemon juice |
| | 0.5 ounce (15 ml) Wineberry Syrup |

Chill a coupe glass.

Skewer the fresh wineberries on a small wooden skewer and set aside for garnishing.

Add the gin, aquafaba, lemon juice, and syrup to a cocktail shaker. Fill the shaker with ice and shake for 8 to 10 seconds to chill. Strain, discard the ice, return the cocktail to the shaker, and dry shake vigorously for 8 to 10 seconds to generate a foam. Pour into the chilled glass. Garnish with the skewered berries.

## WINEBERRY SYRUP

Makes about 1 cup (240 ml)

**1 cup (120 g) fresh wineberries**

**½ cup (100 g) sugar**

Combine the wineberries and sugar with ½ cup (120 ml) water in a medium saucepan and cook over medium heat, stirring occasionally, until the berries start to break down, about 4 minutes.

Let the mixture cool for about 5 minutes, then transfer to a blender and blend until smooth. Strain through a fine-mesh strainer, discarding the solids. Store the syrup in an airtight container in the fridge for up to 5 days.

# MR. FROND

"Nobody wants a relatable guidance counselor."—Mr. Frond

Mr. Frond is the hapless guidance counselor on the animated TV show *Bob's Burgers*. Named both for its namesake's excitable energy and the feathery fennel fronds that make up its garnish, this drink is one of my favorite summertime sips.—*Brian*

| | |
|---|---|
| 1 ounce (30 ml) Banhez mezcal | 0.5 ounce (15 ml) lime juice |
| 0.75 ounce (22 ml) Bonal gentian | Fennel frond |
| 0.75 ounce (22 ml) Fennel Liqueur | Lime wheel |

Add the mezcal, gentian, liqueur, and lime juice to a cocktail shaker. Fill the shaker with ice and shake for 8 to 10 seconds. Strain through a Hawthorne strainer held over a conical strainer into a double rocks glass with a large ice cube. Garnish with the fennel frond and the lime wheel.

## FENNEL LIQUEUR

Makes about 1 cup (240 ml)

| | |
|---|---|
| ½ cup (120 ml) Everclear | 1½ teaspoons chopped orange peel |
| ¼ large fennel bulb, chopped | 1 tablespoon fennel seeds |
| 1 tablespoon cold water | ½ cup (120 ml) Simple Syrup (page 10) |

Make a tincture by combining the Everclear, chopped fennel, cold water, and orange peel in a small bowl. Cover and store in the fridge for at least 6 hours or ideally overnight.

Toast the fennel seeds in a dry saucepan over medium heat just until fragrant, about 3 minutes. Add the simple syrup and cook for 3 minutes, adjusting the heat as necessary to prevent the syrup from boiling. Remove from the heat and strain through a fine-mesh strainer, discarding the solids. Let the syrup cool completely before storing it in an airtight container in the fridge for up to 1 week.

After the tincture has rested, strain it through a fine-mesh strainer, discarding the solids. Combine the tincture with the syrup. Store the liqueur in an airtight container in the fridge for up to 1 week.

# STRAWBERRY SMASH

The best things in life are free—and that includes strawberries, if you know where to pick 'em! If you're picking from June-bearing varietals, this cocktail is the only thing you'll want to drink throughout the month of June. If you have ever-bearing varietals, you can sip this cocktail all summer long. We recommend using gin here, but vodka is a good alternative. Almost any kind of refreshing bubbly soda will work, but we especially like this with Georgian tarragon lemonade.—*Brian*

5 mint leaves

2 large strawberries

1.5 ounces (45 ml) Beefeater gin

0.5 ounce (15 ml) Simple Syrup (page 10)

0.5 ounce (15 ml) lemon juice

3 ounces (90 ml) lemon-lime soda, ginger beer, or Georgian tarragon lemonade

Mint cap

Tarragon sprig

Add the mint and strawberries to a cocktail shaker and muddle until the strawberries are crushed and the mint is well bruised.

Add the gin, syrup, lemon juice, and ½ cup (100 g) ice and shake for 8 to 10 seconds.

Without straining, pour the cocktail into a double rocks glass, top off with fresh ice, then top with the soda. Garnish with the mint cap and tarragon sprig.

**UN-SPIKE IT**    Leave out the gin to make this a fruity nonalcoholic soda.

# LIMA BEAN PISTOU ON TOAST

Serves 4

In summer, when basil is at its peak and the first pole beans are dangling from their vines, this dish is pure French-countryside heaven. If you can't find fresh lima beans, then favas or even green peas will do. And if you make this dish later in the summer, we recommend that you add a thick slice of ripe, juicy tomato between the toast and the pistou.—*Rich*

---

**2 cups (375 g) shelled fresh lima beans**

**3 cups (180 g) lightly packed basil leaves**

**6 garlic cloves, chopped**

**2 tablespoons nutritional yeast**

**¾ cup (180 ml) olive oil**

**1 teaspoon salt**

**1 teaspoon pepper**

**4 thick slices of bread, toasted**

**1 teaspoon flaky salt**

**Lemon wedges**

Bring a pot of salted water to a boil over high heat. Add the lima beans and cook just until tender, 2 to 4 minutes. Drain immediately and set aside.

Combine the basil, garlic, and nutritional yeast with ¼ cup (60 ml) water in a food processor. Pulse while slowly streaming in the olive oil until the basil is fully broken down and the mixture is smooth, about 20 seconds. Add the lima beans and the salt and pepper and pulse a few times to incorporate. The texture should be creamy and slightly chunky.

Spread one quarter of the pistou on each slice of toast. Sprinkle with the flaky salt and serve with lemon wedges on the side.

 **PAIR WITH . . . Mr. Frond** (page 78) for an equally aromatic complement to this herby dish.

# IF YOU'RE GIN, I'M TONIC

I once signed an email to my grandmother, "love, Gin," a new nickname I was trying out. She replied, "If you're gin, I'm tonic," and has signed all her emails, "love, Tonic," ever since. This gin and tonic is an homage both to her and to the cocktail culture in Madrid, where the G&Ts are served in large wine glasses rather than tall Collins glasses, and it's not uncommon to see multiple G&Ts on a drink menu, each formulated to highlight a different gin. Full of dried spices, it's the drink I reach for when I'm craving something refreshing and aromatic.—*Ginevra*

**3 ounces (90 ml) soda water**

**1.5 ounces (45 ml) Citadelle gin**

**0.5 ounce (15 ml) Cocchi Americano**

**0.5 ounce (15 ml) Tonic Syrup (page 85)**

**Juniper berries**

**Fresh lavender sprig**

**Lime peel**

Add the soda water, gin, Cocchi Americano, and syrup to a large wine glass and stir gently to combine. Fill the glass with ice and garnish with the juniper berries, lavender, and lime peel.

## TONIC SYRUP

Makes about ¾ cup (180 ml)

**1 grapefruit, zested and juiced to yield ½ cup (120 ml) juice**

**3 limes, zested and juiced to yield ¼ cup (60 ml) juice**

**2 tablespoons cinchona bark**

**2 tablespoons dried lavender**

**2 cinnamon sticks**

**2 whole star anise**

**10 whole allspice berries**

**¼ cup (50 g) sugar**

**¼ teaspoon citric acid or lemon juice**

Add the grapefruit juice and zest, lime juice and zest, cinchona bark, lavender, cinnamon, star anise, and allspice berries to a medium pot. Bring to a boil over high heat, then remove from the heat and strain the mixture through a fine-mesh strainer lined with cheesecloth, discarding the solids.

Add the sugar and citric acid and stir just until the sugar is dissolved. Store the tonic syrup in an airtight container in the fridge for up to 2 weeks.

# STRAWBERRY PAVLOVETTES

Serves 6 to 8

Used in everything from frothy whiskey sours to sky-high lemon meringue pies, chewy macarons to these mini pavlovas, aquafaba—the water from a can of chickpeas—has proved itself to be an almost miraculous plant-based alternative to egg whites. Light and crisp, these pavlovettes are the perfect cookie canvases for fresh, juicy summer berries.—*Kate*

⅓ cup (80 ml) aquafaba

½ teaspoon lemon juice

⅔ cup (125 g) fine granulated sugar

1 teaspoon vanilla extract

½ teaspoon ground pink peppercorns

1 recipe Strawberry Glaze

1 cup (150 g) fresh strawberries, hulled and quartered

Preheat the oven to 250°F (120°C) and line a baking sheet with parchment paper.

Add the aquafaba to a large metal bowl and beat with a hand mixer on high speed until white and fluffy, about 5 minutes. Add the lemon juice and beat for 2 minutes. Slowly add the sugar while beating for another 2 minutes. (The meringue will deflate slightly when the sugar is added, but it should fluff back up and begin to look shiny with continued beating). Add the vanilla extract and ground peppercorns and beat for another 30 seconds.

Using a large spoon, gently place 12 dollops of meringue onto the prepared baking sheet, leaving at least 2 inches (5 cm) in between.

Reduce the oven temperature to 200°F (95°C) and bake the meringues for 60 minutes. Rotate the baking sheet and then bake another 90 minutes.

Turn off the oven and prop the door ajar with a wooden spoon, allowing the meringues to cool gradually for 30 minutes.

Remove the baking sheet from oven and allow the meringues to cool completely. (The cooled meringues can be stored in an airtight container at room temperature for up to 2 days.)

To serve, arrange the meringues on a plate, gently crack the tops with the back of a spoon, drizzle with the strawberry glaze, and garnish with the fresh strawberries.

# STRAWBERRY GLAZE

Makes about 2 cups (480 ml)

**3 cups (450 g) fresh strawberries, hulled and quartered**

**¼ cup (50 g) sugar**

**½ teaspoon agar powder**

Add the strawberries, sugar, agar powder, and ½ cup (120 ml) water to a blender and blend until smooth.

Strain the mixture through a fine-mesh strainer into a small saucepan. Heat the mixture over high heat until it comes to a boil, then reduce the heat to medium and simmer just until it thickens, about 3 minutes.

Remove from the heat and let the glaze cool completely. Store it in an airtight container in the fridge for up to 5 days.

 **PAIR WITH . . . Strawberry Smash** (page 81) at an afternoon tea party for full berry appreciation.

Strawberry Pavlovettes
served with a
Strawberry Smash

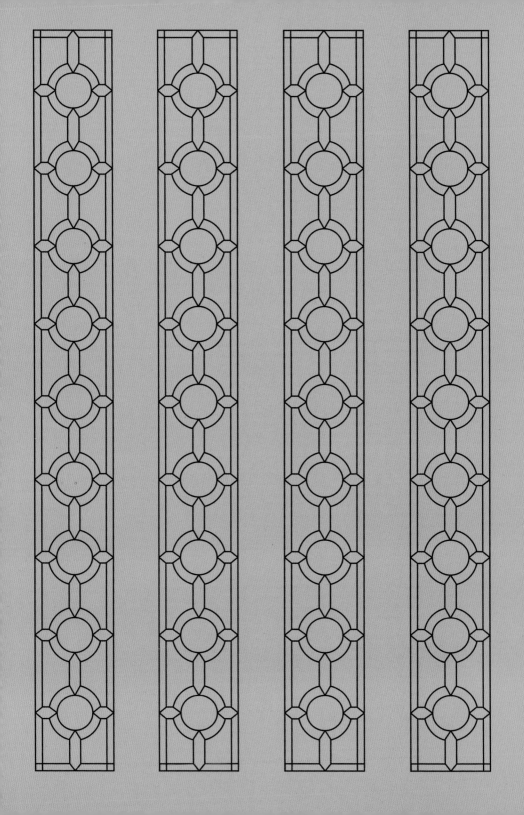

# LATE SUMMER

## Drinks

## Snacks

Late summer, from the third week of August through the fall equinox, is the best time of year to visit the farmers' market. Late summer means blackberries, blueberries, raspberries, freestone peaches, and figs. Tomatoes, sweet corn, ground cherries, pears, and peppers are all at their peak. It means bushes of basil, puffed-up like mini trees, having captured all the summer's sun. Late summer means cocktails that smell of earth and the vibrant ripe fruits that have soaked up the hot sunshine and are now ready to give us back those rays in an elixir of acids and sugars.

These are the days of excess, of bounty and unbridled access before the decline into fall. Late summer feels like it will last forever, encouraging indolence, making us completely forget the coming hush of winter. It's the buzzing of bees and flashing of fireflies before nature takes her long nap.

We can't help but wish to capture some of this overwhelming abundance in our cocktails. In this chapter you'll find drinks that reflect the mood of the season: rich with fruit and a little lazy, relaxed like a cool summer night.

The drink I cannot get enough of this season is the Smoked Corn Silk Old Fashioned (page 97). It's sweet, savory, and smoky—the kind of spirit-forward drink that's perfect for a late summer evening. The Fig Leaf Bourbon Sour (page 120) is another favorite that leans into using parts of the plant that would otherwise go to waste—our way of honoring and savoring summer's bounty.

—Ginevra

# EVEN COWGIRLS GET THE BLUES

In the dog days of summer, we call on juicy blueberries to soften up rough-and-ready whiskey, as well as a little lemon for brightness. We'll all be singin' a different tune after one or two of these.—*Brian*

1.5 ounces (45 ml) Rittenhouse Rye

0.75 ounce (22 ml) Blueberry Syrup

0.75 ounce (22 ml) lemon juice

0.5 ounce (15 ml) Punt e Mes vermouth

Chamomile flower or other edible flower

Chill a coupe glass.

Add the rye, syrup, lemon juice, and vermouth to a cocktail shaker. Fill the shaker with ice and shake for 8 to 10 seconds. Strain through a Hawthorne strainer held over a conical strainer into the chilled glass. Garnish with the chamomile flower.

## BLUEBERRY SYRUP
### Makes about 1 cup (240 ml)

1 cup (150 g) fresh blueberries

½ cup (100 g) sugar

¼ teaspoon citric acid or lemon juice

Add the blueberries, sugar, citric acid, and ½ cup (120 ml) water to a small saucepan and cook over medium heat, stirring occasionally, just until the berries have popped, about 8 minutes.

Remove from the heat and strain through a fine-mesh strainer, pressing gently with the back of a spoon to extract as much syrup as possible. (Reserve the berries for another use, such as topping ice cream.) Let the syrup cool completely before storing it in an airtight container in the fridge for up to 1 week.

# SMOKED CORN SILK OLD FASHIONED

Corn is truly the highlight of late summer. I never grow tired of sweet summer corn, and at Vedge we get some of the best corn in the world from our neighboring state New Jersey. Featuring corn whiskey, corn syrup, and a garnish of smoked corn silk, this drink is both a celebration of the season and a perfect transition into the next.—*Ginevra*

2 ounces (60 ml) Mellow Corn whiskey

0.25 ounce (7 ml) Smoked Corncob Syrup

2 dashes Bittermens Xocolatl Mole Bitters

Smoked corn silk

Add the whiskey, syrup, and bitters to a double rocks glass over a large ice cube. Stir until chilled and diluted. Garnish with the smoked corn silk.

## SMOKED CORNCOB SYRUP

Makes about 3¼ cups (840 ml)

4 ears corn, still in their husks

1½ cups (360 ml) agave syrup or 1½ cups (300 g) sugar

Preheat the oven to 300°F (150°C) and line a baking sheet with parchment paper. Peel back the husks without removing them entirely, then remove the corn silk. Cut away any dark pieces of husk.

Place the corn silk onto the prepared sheet and bake for about 15 minutes, just until the silk is dry. Then smoke the corn silk in a 175°F (80°C) smoker for about 20 minutes. Alternatively, use a blowtorch to toast the silk, or use tongs to carefully hold it above the flame of a gas burner until lightly charred, but note that the silk won't pick up as much smoky flavor. Store in an airtight container and use within 2 days.

Pull the husks back over the ears of corn to cover them and grill over medium-high heat for about 15 minutes, until tender. Let cool, then remove the husks and cut the corn off the cobs. (Reserve the corn for another use.)

Place the corncobs in a large oven-safe casserole dish or roasting pan and pour over 4 cups (960 ml) water. Place in the oven and bake for 3 hours. Remove from the oven and let cool completely, then remove the corncobs and strain the water. Stir in the agave syrup. Store the syrup in an airtight container in the fridge for up to 5 days.

# OLIVES IN TOMATO-CAPER BAGNA CAUDA

Serves 6 to 8

Olives are the perfect cocktail food; they're one of the very few snacks that can be served both in a drink as well as on the side of one. In this recipe, olives go swimming in a bright and herbaceous bagna cauda, or warm oil bath. We like to use pitted Castelvetrano olives here, but any firm large green olive will work. For olive aficionados and purists, it's hard to recommend buying pitted olives, but considering how oily the sauce is, they do work best here, as the centers fill with the extra sauce and flavor the olive from the inside out.—*Rich*

½ cup (120 ml) olive oil

½ cup (90 g) chopped tomato

½ cup (30 g) lightly packed parsley

¼ cup (30 g) capers, drained

1 tablespoon chopped shallot

1 tablespoon Dijon mustard

1 tablespoon sherry vinegar

2 garlic cloves, chopped

1 teaspoon salt

1 teaspoon pepper

2 cups (270 g) pitted Castelvetrano olives

Combine the oil, tomato, parsley, capers, shallot, mustard, vinegar, garlic, salt, and pepper in a food processor and pulse until you have a chunky vinaigrette, about 1 minute.

Transfer the vinaigrette to a medium saucepan and gently warm over low heat for 3 minutes, then pour over the olives and serve.

 **PAIR WITH...** La Tomatina (page 119) to balance this salty dish with a douse of hydration.

# FASCINATOR

Tropical. Spicy. Whiskey sour. Say no more, just pass me another. The sweetness and powerful structure of the bourbon contrast with sour passion fruit and the habanero's heat. To save work, we make our passion fruit syrup with a lightly sweetened store-bought passion fruit puree like Les Vergers Boiron.—*Brian*

1.5 ounces (45 ml) Wild Turkey 101 bourbon

0.75 ounce (15 ml) Passion Fruit Syrup

0.5 ounce (22 ml) lemon juice

0.5 ounce (15 ml) aquafaba

2 dashes Habanero Tincture (page 102)

Pink Peppercorn Salt

Chill a coupe glass.

Add the bourbon, syrup, lemon juice, aquafaba, and habanero tincture to a cocktail shaker. Fill the shaker with ice and shake for 8 to 10 seconds to chill. Strain, discard the ice, return the cocktail to the shaker, and dry shake vigorously for 8 to 10 seconds to generate a foam.

Pour into the chilled glass and sprinkle some of the pink peppercorn salt over the top as a garnish.

## PASSION FRUIT SYRUP

Makes about 1 cup (240 ml)

½ cup (120 ml) passion fruit puree

⅓ cup (65 g) sugar

Small pinch of salt

Add the passion fruit, sugar, salt, and ⅓ cup (80 ml) water to a blender and blend until the sugar is dissolved. Store in an airtight container in the fridge for up to 5 days.

## PINK PEPPERCORN SALT

Makes about 2 tablespoons

2 tablespoons whole pink peppercorns

1 teaspoon coarse kosher salt

1 teaspoon sugar

Add the peppercorns, salt, and sugar to a spice grinder and grind until well combined but still a bit coarse.

Store in an airtight container at room temperature for up to 1 month.

# OUT OF POCKET

Some of our regulars like us to surprise them with something off the menu. That's how this drink, made with the peach shrub we'd been developing at the time along with a few other off-the-cuff additions, came about. Every once in a while, the improvisation becomes a new signature. —*Brian*

1.5 ounces (45 ml) Mistral pisco

0.5 ounce (15 ml) Clément Blanc Rhum Agricole

0.5 ounce (15 ml) Quick Peach Shrub

1 teaspoon Giffard Crème de Cacao

2 dashes Jerry Thomas' Own Decanter bitters

2 dashes Habanero Tincture

Mint cap

Add the pisco, Rhum Agricole, shrub, crème de cacao, bitters, and habanero tincture to a mixing glass. Fill the glass with ice and stir until chilled, 8 to 10 seconds. Strain into a double rocks glass with a large ice cube. Garnish with the mint cap.

## QUICK PEACH SHRUB
Makes about 1 cup (240 ml)

1 large peach, pitted and thinly sliced

½ cup (100 g) sugar

2 teaspoons champagne vinegar

Combine the peach slices and sugar with ½ cup (120 ml) water in a medium saucepan and cook over medium heat, stirring occasionally, until the sugar is dissolved, the peach slices have broken down, and the water has turned dark pink, about 5 minutes.

Let the mixture cool slightly, then strain through a fine-mesh strainer. (Reserve the peaches for another use, such as topping ice cream.) Stir in the vinegar, then let the mixture cool completely before storing it in an airtight container in the fridge for up to 1 week.

## HABANERO TINCTURE
Makes about ½ cup (120 ml)

½ cup (120 ml) Everclear

1 habanero chile, stemmed, seeded, and chopped

Combine the Everclear and chile in an airtight container and let rest in the fridge for at least 12 hours or ideally 48 hours.

Strain the mixture through a fine-mesh strainer, discarding the solids. The tincture will keep in an airtight container in the fridge for at least 1 week.

# IZAKAYA MIX

Serves 6 to 8

Convivial and casual, izakaya (Japanese pubs) traditionally offer otsumami, snacks to enjoy with beer and other drinks. Here we make a custom mix by combining several salty, crunchy favorites. Our preferred shichimi togarashi blends have just a touch of spice and dried citrus. If you can't find shichimi togarashi at the store, you can make your own using dried seaweed, sesame seeds, and a pinch of chili powder and dehydrated citrus peel.—*Rich*

---

**2 cups (240 g) toasted pumpkin seeds**

**2 cups (180 g) salted sesame sticks**

**2 cups (180 g) dry roasted edamame**

**2 cups (120 g) nori rice crackers**

**2 tablespoons shichimi togarashi**

**1 tablespoon nori powder**

**½ teaspoon white pepper**

**¼ teaspoon wasabi powder**

Mix the pumpkin seeds, sesame sticks, edamame, rice crackers, shichimi togarashi, nori powder, pepper, and wasabi powder together in a medium bowl. Store in an airtight container at room temperature for up to 1 week.

 **PAIR WITH...** **Last Dragon** (page 113) for a refreshing, fragrant, and creamy accompaniment to these salty snacks.

# CHICHA MORADA

Outsiders may think of the Pisco Sour as Peru's national drink, but when it comes to everyday sipping, Chicha Morada is actually significantly more popular. Rivaling sales of Coca-Cola in the region, this purple corn–based beverage is a delightful, silky refresher loaded with spices and tropical flavors.—*Ginevra*

**2 ounces (60 ml) Chicha Morada Syrup**

**Freshly chopped pineapple, green apple, and quince**

**Lime wedge**

Combine the syrup with 4 ounces (120 ml) water in a Collins glass and fill with ice. Garnish with the chopped fruit and lime wedge.

## CHICHA MORADA SYRUP

Makes about 1 quart (1 L)

**2 cups (330 g) chopped golden pineapple**

**0.5 pound (225 g) dried Peruvian purple corn on the cob**

**¼ cup plus 2 tablespoons (90 ml) lime juice (about 3 limes)**

**¼ cup (30 g) chopped green apple**

**¼ cup (30 g) chopped quince**

**6 whole cloves**

**1 cinnamon stick**

**1 pound (450 g) sugar**

Combine the pineapple, corn, lime juice, apple, quince, cloves, and cinnamon stick in a large stock pot over medium heat. Bring to a boil and then simmer for 90 minutes, stirring occasionally, until the liquid has noticeably reduced and thickened.

Carefully strain through a large fine-mesh strainer, pressing on the mixture with the back of a spoon to extract as much liquid as possible. Discard the solids.

Return the liquid to the pot, add the sugar, and simmer over medium-low heat until thick and syrupy, about 30 minutes.

Remove from the heat and let the mixture cool completely before storing it in an airtight container in the fridge for up to 1 week.

 **SPIKE IT** You can turn this drink into a pisco fizz by combining 0.75 ounce (22 ml) of the chicha morada syrup with 1 ounce (30 ml) aged pisco, 1 ounce (30 ml) Mexican rum, 0.75 ounce (22 ml) lime juice, and 0.5 ounce (15 ml) aquafaba in a cocktail shaker. Fill the shaker with ice and shake for 8 to 10 seconds, then strain, discard the ice, return the cocktail to the shaker, and dry shake vigorously for 8 to 10 seconds. Pour into a chilled coupe glass. Top with 1 ounce (30 ml) soda water, 2 dashes of Angostura bitters, and garnish with lime zest and an apple wheel.

# U GOT IT BAD

Yes, this cocktail's name is inspired by the Usher song. Like Usher getting steamy, summer heat makes you sweat, so this drink is here to help you cool off. We like to use a mixture of serrano and habanada (habaneros without the heat) chiles in the chile syrup, but you can use any chiles you prefer.—*Brian*

2 ounces (60 ml) Libélula
Joven tequila

0.5 ounce (15 ml) lime juice

0.5 ounce (15 ml) Chile
Pepper Syrup

Four 1-inch (2.5 cm) watermelon cubes

2 ounces (60 ml) soda water

Chile pepper ring

Bachelor button or other edible
flower, optional

Chill a Collins glass.

Add the tequila, lime juice, syrup, and watermelon to a cocktail shaker. Fill the shaker with ice and shake for 8 to 10 seconds. Strain into the chilled glass. Top with the soda water and garnish with the pepper ring and bachelor button, if using.

## CHILE PEPPER SYRUP

Makes about ½ cup (120 ml)

2 to 3 fresh chiles, stemmed, seeded, and chopped

½ cup (100 g) sugar

Toss the chiles with the sugar to coat. Cover and let rest for at least 6 hours or ideally overnight.

Combine the chile-sugar mixture and ½ cup (120 ml) water in a small saucepan and heat over medium heat, stirring until the sugar is dissolved, about 5 minutes.

Strain through a fine-mesh strainer. (Reserve the chiles for another use; they're great dehydrated.) Store the syrup in an airtight container in the fridge for up to 1 week.

# SKEWERED SHIITAKES
## with Buttered Corn Sauce

*Serves 4 to 6*

Late summer is the last hurrah for corn, and this recipe, featuring corn kernels swimming in a corn butter, is about as good a send-off we can imagine. The creamy, smoky corn sauce is impossible to resist. We like to slather it over grilled shiitake mushrooms, but any mushrooms will do here. In fact, try any grilled vegetable— even corn on the cob to double down on the corn flavor.—*Rich*

---

**4 ears corn, shucked**

**¼ cup plus 2 tablespoons (90 ml) sunflower or vegetable oil**

**2 tablespoons tamari**

**2 teaspoons sherry vinegar**

**2 garlic cloves, chopped**

**1 teaspoon Dijon mustard**

**1 teaspoon pepper**

**20 large shiitake mushrooms, stems removed**

**1 cup (225 g) vegan butter**

**½ cup (110 g) vegan mayonnaise**

**2 tablespoons chopped scallions**

**2 teaspoons chipotle chile powder**

**1½ teaspoons salt**

Heat the grill on high and coat the corn with 2 tablespoons of the oil. Grill the corn until golden brown on all sides and starting to char, about 3 minutes. Remove from the heat, shave off kernels, and set aside.

Add the tamari, vinegar, garlic, mustard, pepper, and remaining oil to a bowl and stir to combine. Toss the mushrooms in the marinade to coat, and then thread the mushrooms onto skewers, 3 to 4 mushrooms per skewer. (If you're using wooden or bamboo skewers, make sure to soak them for about 30 minutes first.)

Grill the mushrooms for 2 to 3 minutes on each side or until they have a little bit of char on them, then remove from the heat.

Add half of the corn, the butter, and ½ cup (120 ml) water to a saucepan over medium heat. Simmer for 5 minutes, then remove from the heat and let the mixture steep for 20 minutes. Transfer to a blender and pulse just until the corn is broken down but not pureed, about 5 pulses.

Push the corn mixture through a colander or large-mesh strainer (a fine-mesh strainer will hold back too much pulp). Discard the solids left in the strainer.

Combine the strained liquid with the remaining whole corn kernels, mayonnaise, scallions, chipotle powder, and salt.

Spoon ¼ cup (70 ml) of the corn sauce onto a plate and top with one of the mushroom skewers. Repeat with the remaining skewers. Serve the extra sauce on the side so guests can spoon more over the mushrooms as desired.

**PAIR WITH ... Smoked Corn Silk Old Fashioned** (page 97), because there's no such thing as too much corn.

# LAST DRAGON

St. George is the name of both the legendary soldier said to have slain the last of the dragons and the basil-forward eau de vie that serves as this cocktail's elegant foundation. Basil is at its most abundant in late summer, and this cocktail embraces its floral fragrance with a double hit from the St. George and a fresh basil leaf garnish.—*Brian*

1 ounce (30 ml) Tanqueray No. Ten gin

0.75 ounce (22 ml) St. George basil Eau de Vie

0.75 ounce (22 ml) lemon juice

0.5 ounce (15 ml) Pierre Ferrand Dry Curaçao

0.5 ounce (15 ml) Demerara Syrup

0.5 ounce (15 ml) aquafaba

0.25 ounce (7 ml) Ginger Syrup

Basil leaf

Chill a coupe glass.

Add the gin, eau de vie, lemon juice, curaçao, demerara syrup, aquafaba, and ginger syrup to a cocktail shaker. Fill the shaker with ice and shake for 8 to 10 seconds to chill. Strain, discard the ice, return the cocktail to the shaker, and dry shake vigorously for 8 to 10 seconds to generate a foam. Pour into the chilled glass. Garnish with the basil leaf.

## DEMERARA SYRUP

Makes about ½ cup (120 ml)

1 cup (200 g) demerara sugar

Small pinch of salt

Combine the sugar and salt with ½ cup (120 ml) water in a small saucepan over medium heat, stirring occasionally until the sugar dissolves, about 5 minutes.

Let cool completely, then store in an airtight container in the fridge for up to 2 weeks.

## GINGER SYRUP

Makes about ½ cup (120 ml)

2-inch (5 cm) piece ginger

¼ cup (50 g) sugar

Small pinch of salt

Juice the ginger using a vegetable juicer. Alternatively, grate the ginger using a box grater and then strain through a fine-mesh strainer, pressing with the back of a spoon to extract as much juice as possible, and discard the solids.

Combine the sugar and salt with the ginger juice and ¼ cup (60 ml) water in a small bowl, and whisk until the sugar is fully dissolved. Store in an airtight container in the fridge for up to 5 days.

# FAIR WIND

For a brief stint, Rich and I were boaters. He loved it, and I tolerated it. Whether cruising the Delaware River or the back bays of Atlantic City, I could never quite relax once our depth finder bottomed out. A bit of solace came from knowing a cocktail awaited me back at the dock. It could have been room temperature rum sipped right from the bottle, for all I cared—but even better for a nervous pirate like me is this blend of subtly smoky tequila, sweet coconut water, white port, and a dash of lime juice. So pack your cooler and sip away.—*Kate*

**1 ounce (30 ml) Libélula Joven tequila**

**1 ounce (30 ml) coconut water**

**0.75 ounce (22 ml) white port**

**0.5 ounce (15 ml) lime juice**

**Lime peel**

Combine tequila, coconut water, port, and lime juice in a cocktail shaker. Fill the shaker with ice and shake for 8 to 10 seconds. Strain into a double rocks glass with a large ice cube. Garnish with the lime peel.

# SICHUAN POPCORN

Serves 4 to 6

Sichuan cuisine is known for its bold spices. The most irreplaceable is the Sichuan peppercorn. Its fragrant spice and tingly, mouth-numbing sensation characterizes many Sichuan dishes; combined with the cuisine's renowned heat, you have a flavor profile called "málà," which helps cool diners in sweltering weather. Here, a sprinkling of ground Sichuan peppercorns and a handful of other warm spices instantly elevates the simplest of bar snacks: popcorn.—*Rich*

---

**2 tablespoons vegetable oil**

**1½ cups (290 g) popcorn kernels**

**2 tablespoons ground Sichuan peppercorns**

**1 teaspoon five-spice powder**

**1 teaspoon cayenne or gochugaru flakes**

**1 teaspoon salt**

**1 teaspoon white pepper**

Add the oil and popcorn kernels to a large pot over high heat and stir. Once the first kernel pops, about 3 minutes, cover the pot and reduce the heat to medium, and shake the pot gently to ensure even popping until it tapers down to about 1 pop every 5 seconds, about 3 minutes.

Combine the peppercorns, five-spice powder, cayenne, salt, and pepper in a jar or small bowl. Sprinkle the spice mixture over the freshly popped popcorn to taste.

**PAIR WITH...** a round of spicy **Fascinators** (page 101) to layer the Sichuan peppercorns' numbing tingle with even more heat.

# LA TOMATINA

La Tomatina is a late-summer festival held in the town of Buñol in Valencia, Spain. Locals gather to throw tomatoes at one another for no reason other than it's fun—a tradition that sounds especially appealing toward the end of summer when there are so many ripe tomatoes you can barely keep afloat. But before you start chucking tomatoes at your friends, we recommend setting aside at least a few for use in this refreshing cocktail.—*Brian*

| | |
|---|---|
| Tomato slice | 2 ounces (60 ml) BCN gin |
| Cucumber ribbon | 0.75 ounce (22 ml) Aperol |
| Three ½-inch (1.25 cm) cucumber slices | 0.5 ounce (15 ml) Salted Tomato Water |
| | 2 dashes orange bitters |

Chill a Nick and Nora glass.

Starting from one edge, roll the tomato slice into a simple rosette, then roll part of the cucumber ribbon around the tomato rosette. Skewer to keep the layers from coming apart and set aside for garnish.

Add the cucumber slices to a mixing glass and muddle lightly. Add the gin, Aperol, tomato water, and bitters, fill the glass with ice, and stir until chilled, 8 to 10 seconds. Strain through a Hawthorne strainer held over a conical strainer into the chilled glass. Garnish with the tomato-cucumber rosette.

## SALTED TOMATO WATER

Makes about ½ cup (120 ml)

**1 tomato, chopped**

**1 teaspoon fine sea salt**

Add the tomato to a small bowl, sprinkle with the salt, and stir to combine. Cover and let rest for 2 hours.

Strain through a fine-mesh strainer. (Be patient; resist pushing the tomato mixture through the strainer, or the liquid will be muddy. Save the chopped tomato for another use.) Store the liquid in an airtight container in the fridge for up to 3 days.

# FIG LEAF BOURBON SOUR

Our local fig trees are bursting at the seams in late summer, and in this cocktail we proudly flaunt their leaves. You read that right: The abundant fruits are great eaten fresh or preserved, but the leaves, too, have culinary uses. With a distinctive grassy and slightly nutty flavor, the leaves, much like bay or lime leaves, can add nuance to your cooking and cocktailing.—*Ginevra*

**1.5 ounces (45 ml) Fig Leaf–Infused Bourbon**

**0.75 ounce (22 ml) lemon juice**

**0.75 ounce (22 ml) Simple Syrup (page 10)**

**0.5 ounce (15 ml) aquafaba**

**Fig leaf**

Chill a coupe glass.

Add the bourbon, lemon juice, simple syrup, and aquafaba to a cocktail shaker. Fill the shaker with ice and shake for 8 to 10 seconds to chill. Strain, discard the ice, return the cocktail to the shaker, and dry shake vigorously for 8 to 10 seconds to generate a foam. Pour into the chilled glass and garnish with the fig leaf.

## FIG LEAF–INFUSED BOURBON

Makes 1½ cups (360 ml)

**2 fig leaves**

**1½ cups (360 ml) Wild Turkey 101 bourbon**

Combine the fig leaves and bourbon in an airtight container and let rest for a minimum of 24 hours or up to 48 hours. Strain through a fine-mesh strainer lined with cheesecloth. The infused bourbon will keep in the fridge for 1 to 2 weeks.

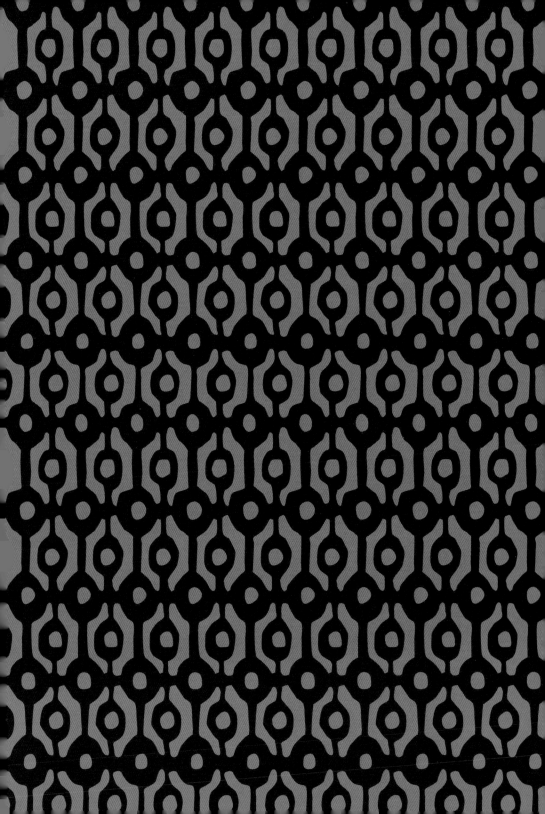

# FALL

## Drinks

## Snacks

## ...fall teaches you to appreciate change, to take stock and value each moment.

In the Northeast and Mid-Atlantic, we endure blazing hot, humid summers and painfully long, gloomy winters. The transitions, though, are generally mild. Spring is a joyous celebration. It's an easy season: Everyone is happy and hopeful. Sunshine on our vitamin D–deficient skin, we thaw and awaken from a long winter slumber. But fall is something else.

My dad used to say that fall was better than spring because the ground was still warm. He was right. We're still warm inside with the glow collected during those long, sunny summer days. But the parties start to die down, and summer's carefree vibes, its days of running around with barely anything on, yield to a buttoned-up back-to-school mode. We cherish the still-warm days as the nights grow longer and cooler. It's time to light a fire and raise a glass of Gamay.

Almost every chef will tell you that fall is the best season for cooking, and bartenders feel it, too. The rustic brush strokes of summer give way to more finely detailed creations, more complex sauces, more prep work, more intricate, layered presentations. While a few summer vegetables continue to hang on, the heartier squashes and leafier greens start showing up. Tender basil gives way to woody rosemary, white wine to red, rum to Scotch. Barefoot hangouts on the beach become intimate gatherings, hosted indoors around formal dining tables. We light candles again. Reggae and country switches to classical and jazz. Thirst-quenching summer drinks are replaced by concentrated boozy concoctions meant to be sipped slowly over great conversation. Everything tastes better as our minds and palates resettle post–summer haze.

All of this, of course, sets the stage running up to the holidays, making fall one of the most satisfying seasons of all, full of gratitude. It's why those of us born in the Northeast so often stay here. More than any other season, fall teaches you to appreciate change, to take stock and value each moment. And a perfect fall day is nothing short of euphoric.

—Rich

# PAPER HEART

Quince was once grown in abundance throughout the United States. This bittersweet drink, our riff on the Paper Plane, which is itself a take on the Last Word, is our attempt to give this now-underappreciated fruit the spotlight it deserves once again.—*Ginevra*

1.5 ounces (45 ml) Brisson VS Cognac

0.75 ounce (22 ml) Quince Syrup

0.5 ounce (15 ml) lemon juice

0.5 ounce (15 ml) Rittenhouse Rye

0.25 ounce (7 ml) Cynar

6 dashes Angostura bitters

Borage, baby marigold, or other edible flowers, optional

Chill a coupe glass.

Combine the cognac, syrup, lemon juice, rye, Cynar, and bitters in a cocktail shaker. Fill the shaker with ice and shake for 8 to 10 seconds. Strain into the chilled glass. Garnish with the borage, if using.

## QUINCE SYRUP

Makes about 1 cup (240 ml)

1 cup (225 g) quince paste (membrillo), chopped

2 teaspoons lemon juice

Pinch of salt

Add the quince paste, lemon juice, salt, and ¾ cup (180 ml) water to a large saucepan over medium heat and cook, stirring occasionally, until the water comes to a boil and the quince paste has fully dissolved, 6 to 8 minutes. Reduce the heat to low and simmer for 10 minutes, until slightly thickened.

Remove from the heat and let cool completely. Store the syrup in an airtight container in the fridge for up to 5 days.

# NORDIC SUNSET

This cocktail was inspired by nimbu pani, a spiced and salted Indian lemonade, and my good friend Davey Jeff, who once called me into the kitchen as he was rinsing a salted purple cabbage to see the magnificent color running off of it. Finessing the drink took some work, but once I'd homed in on the right amount of salt and hit upon the idea of using aquafaba to help absorb the cabbage's somewhat strong smell, I knew I had a real showpiece. Earthy and complex, it's now one of my proudest creations!—*Ginevra*

| | |
|---|---|
| 1 ounce (30 ml) Beefeater gin | 0.5 ounce (15 ml) aquafaba |
| 0.75 ounce (22 ml) Brennivín aquavit | 2 ounces (60 ml) soda water |
| 0.75 ounce (22 ml) Spiced Simple Syrup | 0.25 ounce (7 ml) Purple Cabbage Juice |
| 0.75 ounce (22 ml) lemon juice | |

Chill a Collins glass.

Add the gin, aquavit, simple syrup, lemon juice, and aquafaba to a cocktail shaker. Fill the shaker with ice and shake for 8 to 10 seconds to chill. Strain, discard the ice, return the cocktail to the shaker, and dry shake vigorously for 8 to 10 seconds to generate a foam. Pour into the chilled glass and top with the soda water.

Carefully pour the cabbage juice over the back of a spoon to float the juice just under the foam layer.

## SPICED SIMPLE SYRUP

Makes about 1 cup (240 ml)

| | |
|---|---|
| 2 teaspoons coriander seeds | 2 large or 1 small star anise |
| 4 green cardamom pods | 1 cup (240 ml) Simple Syrup (page 10) |

Add the coriander, cardamom, and star anise to a small saucepan and crack them using a muddler or the back of a large spoon.

Toast the spices over medium-high heat, shaking the saucepan a few times, until they're fragrant, about 2 minutes. Add the syrup and reduce the heat to low, then simmer for 10 minutes, until the flavors meld and the syrup is slightly thickened.

Strain through a fine-mesh strainer, discarding the solids. Store the syrup in an airtight container in the fridge for up to 1 week.

# PURPLE CABBAGE JUICE

Makes about ½ cup (120 ml)

**¼ small head red cabbage, chopped**

**2 teaspoons salt**

Add the cabbage to a medium bowl and sprinkle with the salt. Cover and let rest for 60 minutes.

Juice the cabbage using a vegetable juicer. Alternatively, add the cabbage to a blender with just enough water to engage the blades, about ¼ cup (60 ml). Blend on low, then strain through a fine-mesh strainer, discarding the solids. Store the juice in the fridge for up to 3 days.

# EGGPLANT SKORDALIA

Serves 2 to 4

Greece's skordalia, a rich and garlicky puree of potatoes, bread, and sometimes almonds, may sound heavy, but a good one—like the version Kate and I were once fortunate enough to savor over cold glasses of retsina at the Sunset Ammoudi while vacationing on the island of Santorini—feels surprisingly light. To ours, we've added earthy eggplant for an even creamier texture. (To add a smoky note, try char-grilling the eggplant.) Serve with crostini, freshly sliced veggies, or pita.—*Rich*

---

**1 Yukon Gold or other waxy potato**

**1 medium eggplant**

**1 cup plus 1 tablespoon (255 ml) olive oil**

**2 slices bread, stale or toasted, cubed**

**2 tablespoons sherry vinegar**

**2 garlic cloves**

**2 teaspoons dried oregano**

**1 teaspoon salt**

**1 teaspoon pepper**

**Fresh rosemary sprig**

Preheat the oven to 400°F (200°C). Wrap the potato in foil and bake just until tender, about 60 minutes. Let the potato cool enough to handle, then remove the foil, peel and discard the skin, and cut it into 1-inch (2.5 cm) chunks.

While the potato bakes, peel the eggplant and cut it into 1-inch (2.5 cm) slices, removing any large seed pockets. Toss gently with 1 tablespoon of the oil, then place on a baking sheet and roast until tender, about 15 minutes.

Combine the bread, vinegar, garlic, oregano, salt, and pepper, the baked potato and roasted eggplant pieces, the remaining olive oil, and 1 cup (240 ml) water in a food processor and pulse until smooth, about 3 minutes. Transfer to a serving dish and garnish with the rosemary.

**PAIR WITH** ... an umami-packed cocktail like the **The Underdark** (page 132) that's capable of standing up to the eggplant and pungent garlic.

# THE UNDERDARK

*Through the door you can see the altar, the golden idol gleaming in the single ray of moonlight shining through a miles-long shaft in the rock overhead. Just as you begin to advance, half a dozen armored skeletons shuffle into the room wielding rusty blades. Roll initiative!* ... In D&D, one of my favorite pastimes, the Underdark is a cavernous underground region full of monsters and bioluminescent fungi. This complex, mushroom-infused, revitalizing potion is a drink fit for the bravest adventurers.—*Brian*

| | |
|---|---|
| **1.5 ounces (45 ml) Plymouth Gin** | **1 teaspoon Batavia Arrack rum** |
| **0.75 ounce (22 ml) Dolin Rouge vermouth** | **5 to 6 dashes Lion's Mane Tincture** |
| **0.5 ounce (15 ml) Dolin Génépi** | **1 Mushroom-Stuffed Olive, skewered** |

Chill a Nick and Nora glass.

Add the gin, vermouth, génépi, rum, and tincture to a mixing glass. Fill the glass with ice and stir until chilled, 8 to 10 seconds. Strain into the chilled glass. Garnish with the olive.

## LION'S MANE TINCTURE
### Makes about ⅓ cup (80 ml)

**½ cup (150 g) fresh Lion's Mane mushroom, chopped**

**2.5 ounces (75 ml) Everclear**

Add the mushroom and Everclear to a mason jar and stir to combine. Cover and let rest in the fridge for 1 week, stirring occasionally.

Strain through a fine-mesh strainer lined with cheesecloth, pressing on the solids with the back of a spoon to extract as much liquid as possible.

Add the mushrooms and 2 tablespoons water to a small saucepan and heat over low heat, stirring occasionally, until the mushrooms are soft and swollen, about 15 minutes. Strain through the cheesecloth-lined fine-mesh strainer again, pressing to extract the liquid, and add this liquid to the previously strained tincture. Store the tincture in an airtight container in the fridge for up to 1 week.

# MUSHROOM-STUFFED OLIVES

Makes 24 olives

2 portobello mushrooms,
thinly sliced

1 tablespoon olive oil

½ teaspoon salt

¼ teaspoon pepper

1 tablespoon mirin

24 pitted green olives

Preheat the oven to 425°F (220°C) and line a baking sheet with parchment paper. Place the mushrooms on the prepared baking sheet, toss them in the oil, and sprinkle with the salt and pepper, then roast in the oven until tender, about 15 minutes. Remove the mushroom from the oven, allow to cool for a few minutes, then transfer to a food processor, add the mirin, and pulse until the mushrooms are broken down with some texture remaining.

Transfer the paste to a piping bag and fill the olives. Store in an airtight container in the fridge for up to 1 week.

MONSTER MANUAL

by Gary Gygax

# JACKALOUPE

In the Mid-Atlantic, the seasonal cycle is on best display in fall, when the back-to-school advertisements kick into full gear and bars and cafés are suddenly hawking pumpkin spice everything. This combination of tequila, apple brandy, maple syrup, and refreshing dry hard cider captures the fall spirit in a less clichéd way. Now you just need your favorite flannel, and it's officially fall!—*Kate*

1 ounce (30 ml) Libélula Joven tequila

0.5 ounce (15 ml) Laird's apple brandy

0.5 ounce (15 ml) Oloroso sherry

0.25 ounce (7 ml) lemon juice

0.25 ounce (7 ml) maple syrup

1 ounce (30 ml) dry hard cider

Apple slices

Add the tequila, brandy, sherry, lemon juice, and maple syrup to a cocktail shaker. Fill the shaker with ice and shake for 8 to 10 seconds. Strain into a Collins glass filled with ice. Top with the hard cider and garnish with the apple slice.

# BLISTERED SNACK PEPPERS
## with Creamy Adjika

Serves 4 to 6

Years ago, while preparing a menu for a Georgian wine dinner at Vedge, I found myself utterly entranced by adjika, a creamy sauce of red peppers and walnuts. Here, it serves as a dip for one of my all-time favorite bar snacks: seared peppers. I love to use Padrón peppers when they're in season, but any snack-size pepper, like baby bell peppers or shishitos, will work just fine.—*Rich*

---

1 cup (260 g) jarred roasted red peppers, drained

½ cup (90 g) chopped plum tomato

¼ cup (30 g) chopped walnuts

2 tablespoons olive oil

1 tablespoon lightly packed fresh dill

1 tablespoon vegan sour cream

1 teaspoon sherry vinegar

1 garlic clove

½ teaspoon salt

½ teaspoon pepper

½ teaspoon ground coriander

¼ teaspoon smoked paprika

¼ teaspoon ground fenugreek

1 tablespoon sunflower or vegetable oil

2 cups (300 g) snack peppers, such as Padrón peppers

To make the adjika, add the roasted peppers, tomato, walnuts, oil, dill, sour cream, vinegar, garlic, salt, pepper, coriander, paprika, fenugreek, and 2 tablespoons water to a food processor and pulse until well combined. (The adjika can be stored in an airtight container in the fridge for up to 1 week.)

Heat the sunflower oil in a wok or skillet over high heat. As soon as the oil begins to ripple, add the snack peppers and sear until blistered on one side, about 1 minute, then flip the peppers and sear the other side, about 30 seconds.

Transfer the peppers to a serving dish and serve with the dip on the side.

**PAIR WITH** ... a juicy, lip-smacking cocktail like **Jackaloupe** (page 137) to counter the salt and spice.

# MARTIAN SUNRISE

Human eyes have yet to directly witness a Martian sunrise, but when we imagine the sun's distant rays being scattered through Mars's thin atmosphere, we can't help but think it must look something like this orange-hued drink. Developed to highlight sweet tangerine juice as it becomes available in late fall, the lemon and carbonation give this nonalcoholic soda a boost. So hold on tight and count down for liftoff in 5, 4, 3 . . . —*Brian*

1.5 ounces (45 ml) tangerine juice

1 ounce (30 ml) carrot juice

0.5 ounce (15 ml) lemon juice

0.5 ounce (15 ml) Spiced Simple Syrup (page 128)

1 ounce (30 ml) soda water

Calendula, flowering basil, or other edible flowers, optional

Chill a coupe glass.

Add the tangerine, carrot, and lemon juices and the simple syrup to a cocktail shaker. Fill the shaker with ice and shake for 8 to 10 seconds. Strain into the chilled glass and top with the soda water. Garnish with the calendula, if using.

 **SPIKE IT** For a wilder ride, just add 2 ounces (60 ml) gin or vodka.

# ROSE CHOCOLATE FUDGE

## Serves 8 to 10

Fudge is a decadent cocktail party treat, but it can be intimidating to make. Once you understand the technique, though, it's a beautiful canvas for seasonal ingredients. The cocoa butter in this fudge hints at the flavors of white chocolate and highlights the last rose petals of fall, along with rosemary, which is just hitting its peak as the weather starts to cool.—*Kate*

---

**1 rosemary sprig**

**½ cup (110 g) vegan butter**

**2 cups (400 g) sugar**

**½ cup (120 ml) vegan heavy cream**

**1 tablespoon maple syrup**

**½ cup (100 g) cocoa butter chips**

**2 tablespoons chopped rose petals**

Line a 9 x 13–inch (22 x 32 cm) baking pan that's at least 1 inch (2.5 cm) deep with parchment paper and place in the fridge to chill. Pick 5 to 10 small leaves from the rosemary sprig, chop them finely, and set them aside.

Wipe the sides of a medium saucepan with the butter, then melt the butter in the saucepan over low heat. Add the rosemary sprig and cook for 1 minute, until fragrant. Remove the rosemary, add the sugar, heavy cream, and maple syrup, and stir until the sugar dissolves. Simmer over low heat, without stirring, until the mixture has reduced by half, 25 to 30 minutes. (Stirring will agitate the sugar and cause it to crystallize.) Use a candy thermometer to monitor the temperature of the sugar mixture as it cooks, and adjust the heat as needed to keep the temperature between 234 and 240°F (112–115°C). When the mixture begins to thicken, remove the saucepan from the heat and set aside to cool for 15 to 20 minutes.

When the fudge is still warm but the pan is cool enough to handle, add the cocoa butter and stir with a wooden spoon until it melts, then continue to stir vigorously for 30 seconds to incorporate air into the mixture. The fudge should thicken further and take on a matte sheen. Pour the fudge into the prepared pan, smoothing as needed.

Sprinkle with the rose petals and chopped rosemary, then place the fudge in the fridge and allow to cool completely and set up, about 2 hours, before slicing into 12 pieces and serving. (The fudge can be stored in an airtight container in the fridge for up to 1 week.)

 **PAIR WITH . . . Paper Heart** (page 127) so the smooth booze can cut through the decadent fudge.

# HIGHER FREQUENCY

Able to detect sounds up to ten times higher in pitch than humans, bats excel at using their sensitive hearing to navigate at night. As the daylight hours dwindle, we can only wish to be able to move through the gathering dark as easily as the bats that pollinate the agave plants that go on to produce the smoky mezcal and smooth reposado tequila in this drink. With its apple-sweetness and spice notes, it's the perfect autumnal sipper. Any good baking apple will be excellent in the cordial.—*Brian*

1 ounce (30 ml) Banhez mezcal

0.75 ounce (22 ml) Apple-Fennel Cordial

0.75 ounce (22 ml) lemon juice

0.5 ounce (15 ml) Rejon Reposado tequila

0.5 ounce (15 ml) Cardamaro

2 dashes Angostura bitters

Apple fan, skewered

Chill a coupe glass.

Add the mezcal, cordial, lemon juice, tequila, Cardamaro, and bitters to a cocktail shaker. Fill the shaker with ice and shake for 8 to 10 seconds. Strain into the chilled glass. Garnish with the apple fan.

## APPLE-FENNEL CORDIAL
Makes about 1 cup (240 ml)

2 apples, chopped

¼ fennel bulb, chopped

1 cup (200 g) sugar

Juice the apple and fennel using a vegetable juicer. Alternatively, add the apple and fennel to a blender along with just enough water to engage the blades (about 2 tablespoons) and blend until smooth, then strain through a fine-mesh strainer.

Add the juice to a small saucepan with the sugar and heat over medium heat until the liquid comes to a boil, about 4 minutes. Reduce the heat to low and simmer, using a slotted spoon to skim away any foam that forms on the surface. Keep skimming until the liquid is mostly clear, about 5 minutes.

Remove from the heat, strain through a fine-mesh strainer, and let cool completely. Store the cordial in an airtight container in the fridge for up to 5 days.

# GOLDEN APPLE

Maybe it's the sommelier in me, but I tend to lean heavily on fortified wines and brandies in my cocktailing. This spin on a Turf Club highlights one of my favorite white vermouths for fall, all golden-hued and singing with sunshine. Stir in the power-packed Calvados and garnish with a tumble of fragrant Tangerine Lace, and the first sip will transport you to a local orchard and make you feel like you're rolling around in just-raked leaves.—*Kate*

1 dash La Charlotte absinthe

1 ounce (30 ml) Calvados

1 ounce (30 ml) Vergano White Vermouth

0.25 ounce (7 ml) Dolin Génépi

0.25 ounce (7 ml) St. Germain elderflower liqueur

Sprig of Tangerine Lace or lemon peel

Rinse or atomize (finely spray) a coupe glass with the absinthe. Chill the glass.

Combine the Calvados, vermouth, génépi, and liqueur in a mixing glass. Fill the glass with ice and stir until chilled, 8 to 10 seconds. Strain into the chilled glass. Garnish with the Tangerine Lace.

# HOLIDAY SEASON

## Drinks

**Bay Bae** 152

**Beet Mind Eraser** 155

**Last-Minute Tradition** 159

**Bury the Hatchet** 162

**Great Persuader** 164

**Old Acquaintance** 171

**Pomegranate Boulevardier** 175

## Snacks

**Rutabaga Fondue** 156

**Roasted Maitake Mushrooms
with Jager Sauce** 160

**Deviled Kohlrabi with Green Olives** 167

**Hickory-Pecan Caramel Corn** 168

**Mushroom Tapenade** 172

**H**oliday season is its own entity, not quite fall, not quite winter; the calendar version of Washington, DC, or Vatican City. Kicking off with Thanksgiving and spanning through New Years, it's an intense micro-bubble within the traditional seasonal cycle. By the time holiday season arrives, we've already worked through the last vegetables of the harvest and preserved as much as we possibly could. Now it's time to party!

**We bring batched cocktails to cookie exchanges, and we search for ugly sweaters.**

It's a marathon, but it's also over before you know it. When everyone gets into the spirit, it feels like anything goes. We eat, we drink, we celebrate. Winter is coming, but we don't give a fuck. We're partying! Families visit from out of town. Decorations fill the house. Candles flicker while Charlie Brown and Kevin McCallister prance around on our screens. Wine pours easily. Warm winter cocktails tingle on the way down. Every drink starts with a toast and each meal is a celebration. Champagne is popped "just because." We embark on laborious family traditions, like making a thousand pierogies. And sure, you can shave truffles on that! Why not? We polish our silver and clink our fanciest glassware. We sing along to holiday favorites imprinted in our memories back in childhood. We bring batched cocktails to cookie exchanges, and we search for ugly sweaters. It's a time to imbibe all the holiday cheer. It's a time for generosity and flamboyance. Time too for graciousness and conviviality. The holiday season is all about overindulgence, the last of the Last Calls, if you will. And we wouldn't have it any other way.

—Rich and Kate

# BAY BAE

Meyer lemons are one of our favorite citrus fruits, but they're at their peak for only a short time each year. This festive cocktail showcases their fleeting floral sweetness alongside the mysterious herbal notes of bay leaf, like a fancy French 75 meeting a bouquet garni. Choose whatever sparkling wine you like best; we like using a dry Prosecco.—*Ginevra*

1 ounce (30 ml) Beefeater gin

0.5 ounce (15 ml) Bay Leaf Syrup

0.5 ounce (15 ml) Meyer lemon juice

2 ounces (60 ml) sparkling white wine

Meyer lemon peel

Chill a small wine glass.

Add the gin, syrup, and lemon juice to a cocktail shaker. Fill the shaker with ice and shake for 8 to 10 seconds. Strain into the wine glass and top with the sparkling wine. Garnish with the lemon peel.

## BAY LEAF SYRUP
Makes about ½ cup (120 ml)

½ cup (100 g) sugar

2 small, dried bay leaves or 1 fresh bay leaf

Combine the sugar and bay leaves in a small bowl and muddle until the bay leaves are bruised. Cover and let rest for at least 6 hours or ideally overnight.

Add ½ cup (120 ml) water and stir until the sugar is dissolved. Strain through a fine-mesh strainer, discarding the bay leaves. Store the syrup in an airtight container in the fridge for up to 1 week.

# BEET MIND ERASER

Years ago, when working at a bar decidedly less sophisticated than the one at Vedge, I learned of a holiday that's been all but forgotten by everyone except a few US bartenders: Repeal Day, December 5, the day in 1933 that Prohibition was ended. Ever after, I'd demand to work every December 5 and, around midnight, I'd mix a round of Mind Erasers on the house, cut the music, and drink a toast to our constitutionally guaranteed right to enjoy a good drink—something I still celebrate—now, with a modern, vegetable-forward twist.—*Brian*

1.5 ounces (45 ml) Beet Shrub

0.75 ounce (22 ml) Punt e Mes vermouth

1 ounce (30 ml) Luksusowa Vodka

3 drops vanilla extract

2 ounces (60 ml) soda water

Fill a Collins glass with ice and add a straw. Build distinct layers by individually pouring the shrub, the vermouth, the vodka, the vanilla extract, and the soda water over the ice.

## BEET SHRUB

Makes about 2 cups (480 ml)

2 to 3 red beets (240 g), peeled and finely chopped

1 cup plus 2 tablespoons (225 g) sugar

2 tablespoons apple cider vinegar

Combine the beets, sugar, vinegar, and ¾ cup plus 2 tablespoons (210 ml) water in a small bowl and stir until the sugar dissolves. Cover and let rest in the fridge for at least 8 hours or ideally overnight.

Strain through a fine-mesh strainer. (Save the beets for another use; they're great in a salad.) Store the shrub in an airtight container in the fridge for up to 1 week.

# RUTABAGA FONDUE

Serves 4 to 6

Sometimes journalists ask for our thoughts on the next big vegetable fad. Our answer is always rutabaga. Now that celery root is having its day, we're still lobbying for rutabaga. This root vegetable has flesh that's the color of peaches and a nutty flavor that, when combined with cheesy ingredients like miso and nutritional yeast, takes on a cheddar-like quality. A Vedge staple for years, this fondue is one of our most popular dishes, and we've promised many of our patrons that if we wrote another cookbook, the recipe would be included. So here it is: a home-friendly rutabaga fondue that honors the original we serve at the restaurant. Best served with a soft pretzel!—*Rich*

---

4 cups (560 g) roughly chopped, peeled rutabaga

1 Yukon Gold or other waxy potato, peeled and chopped

¼ cup (40 g) chopped shallot

1 tablespoon chopped garlic

¼ cup (60 ml) sunflower or vegetable oil

1 teaspoon salt

¼ cup (20 g) nutritional yeast

2 tablespoons miso

1 teaspoon white pepper

1½ cups (330 g) vegan mayonnaise or sour cream

Add the rutabaga and potato to a large pot with just enough water to cover. Bring to a boil over high heat and boil just until fork-tender, 8 to 12 minutes. Reserve 2 cups (480 ml) of the cooking water, then drain.

Sauté the shallot and garlic in the oil in a small saucepan over medium heat until golden brown, 2 to 3 minutes. Add the salt, nutritional yeast, miso, and white pepper, stir to combine, and remove from the heat.

Combine the cooked rutabaga and potato, the shallot mixture, and the mayonnaise in a blender. Blend until smooth and creamy. Add the reserved cooking water, a little at a time, if necessary, to make the mixture run smooth; it should be thick but pourable. Serve. (The fondue can be stored in an airtight container in the fridge for up to 3 days. Let it sit at room temperature for about 20 minutes before serving.)

 **PAIR WITH...** a powerful cocktail like **Great Persuader** (page 164) to temper this dish's richness and for a little holiday indulgence.

# LAST-MINUTE TRADITION

Orgeat (think of it as a syrupy almond milk) is a great recipe to have in your bar repertoire, especially over the holidays when boozy, sweet, and creamy drinks reign supreme. In our Last-Minute Tradition, we infuse the orgeat with poached pear for extra fall finesse, and let bourbon and amaro do the heavy lifting. No garnish necessary—this frothy cocktail looks like a grown-up milkshake straight out of the shaker! Feel free to experiment with making the orgeat with other nuts, like pistachios or pecans.—*Brian*

0.75 ounce (22 ml) Maker's Mark bourbon

0.75 ounce (22 ml) Poached Pear–Almond Orgeat

0.5 ounce (15 ml) Amaro Meletti

0.5 ounce (15 ml) lemon juice

0.5 ounce (15 ml) aquafaba

0.25 ounce (7 ml) Booker's barrel-strength bourbon

0.25 ounce (7 ml) pear brandy

0.25 ounce (7 ml) Simple Syrup (page 10)

Chill a rocks glass.

Add the Maker's Mark bourbon, orgeat, amaro, lemon juice, aquafaba, Booker's bourbon, brandy, and simple syrup to a cocktail shaker. Fill the shaker with ice and shake for 8 to 10 seconds to chill. Strain, discard the ice, return the cocktail to the shaker, and dry shake vigorously for 8 to 10 seconds to generate a foam. Pour into the chilled glass.

## POACHED PEAR–ALMOND ORGEAT

Makes about 1 cup (240 ml)

2 pears, peeled, cored and cut into 1-inch (2.5 cm) cubes

½ cup (75 g) unsalted roasted almonds

½ cup (100 g) sugar

Pinch of salt

Add the pears and 1 cup (240 ml) water to a medium saucepan over medium heat and cook just until the pears are tender, about 10 minutes. Remove the pears from the pan and reserve the poaching liquid.

Pulse the almonds in a food processor until finely chopped. Add the sugar and pulse again to form a rough paste. Add the poached pears and the salt and, while processing, slowly stream in half the poaching liquid until the mixture is smooth and pourable. Add a bit more poaching liquid if necessary.

Strain the mixture through a fine-mesh strainer lined with a coffee filter or cheesecloth. Store the orgeat in an airtight container in the fridge for up to 5 days.

# ROASTED MAITAKE MUSHROOMS
## with Jager Sauce

Serves 4

While doing some crash research for an Austrian-themed wine dinner we held at Vedge, I, a gatherer, found myself ironically drawn to Jager ("hunter") sauce. While Jager sauce is technically German, it prevails all over Eastern Europe, and this version featuring savory wild mushrooms is hearty and perfect for winter. You can substitute ¼ cup (60 g) of vegan sour cream for the heavy cream if you like. If you can't find Montreal Steak Seasoning, you can approximate it with equal parts kosher salt, pepper, paprika, garlic powder, onion powder, coriander, dill, and cayenne. Serve on crostini or toast triangles, or make it an entree by serving it over pilaf or wild rice.—*Rich*

---

¼ cup (60 ml) sunflower or vegetable oil

1 tablespoon chopped garlic

½ cup (80 g) finely chopped onion

2 cups (170 g) chopped oyster or Lion's Mane mushrooms

1½ teaspoons pepper

1 teaspoon salt

1 teaspoon porcini powder

1 teaspoon Montreal Steak Seasoning (see headnote)

¼ cup (60 ml) white wine

2 tablespoons Madeira

¾ cup (180 ml) vegetable stock

½ cup (120 ml) vegan heavy cream

2 tablespoons vegan butter

1 teaspoon Dijon mustard

2 pounds (900 g) maitake mushrooms

2 teaspoons chopped fresh thyme

1 teaspoon chopped fresh rosemary

Heat a large skillet over high heat with 2 tablespoons of the oil, then sauté the garlic, onion, and oyster mushrooms until they start to brown, about 8 minutes. Add 1 teaspoon of the pepper, the salt, porcini powder, and steak seasoning, and stir to combine.

Deglaze the pan with the white wine and Madeira, reduce the heat to medium, and continue to cook until the sauce's volume has reduced by half, about 2 minutes. Add the stock and bring to a boil.

Remove from the heat, stir in the cream, butter, and mustard, and let the butter melt.

Heat the remaining oil in a large sauté pan over high heat and sear the maitakes on one side until crispy, about 2 minutes. Flip the mushrooms and sear on the other side, about 1 minute. Sprinkle with the remaining pepper, then remove from the heat.

Arrange the maitakes on a serving dish. Stir the fresh herbs into the sauce and serve alongside the seared maitakes.

 **PAIR WITH . . . Pomegranate Boulevardier** (page 175). Its tart high notes will shine against the savory mushrooms.

# BURY THE HATCHET

We all gather together for the holidays—and sometimes with people we'd rather not. But perhaps this holiday season we can find it within ourselves to lift a vibrant cranberry-infused glass and make peace. To paraphrase the Cranberries, don't let the bad feelings linger.—*Brian*

**2 small sprigs rosemary**

**3 dashes lemon bitters**

**2 ounces (60 ml) Wild Turkey 101 bourbon**

**0.75 ounce (22 ml) Cranberry-Miso Shrub**

**1 Candied Cranberry, skewered**

Chill a rocks glass.

Add 1 sprig of rosemary and the lemon bitters to a mixing glass and muddle gently. Add the bourbon and shrub, fill the glass with ice, and stir until chilled, 8 to 10 seconds. Strain through a Hawthorne strainer held over a conical strainer into the chilled glass. Garnish with the candied cranberry and the remaining rosemary sprig.

# CRANBERRY-MISO SHRUB

Makes about 1 cup (240 ml)

½ cup (50 g) fresh cranberries

2 teaspoons white miso

½ cup (100 g) sugar

1 teaspoon balsamic vinegar

¼ teaspoon citric acid or lemon juice

Combine the cranberries and miso with ½ cup (120 ml) water in a medium saucepan over medium heat. Bring to a boil, reduce the heat to low, and simmer until the cranberries have popped, about 7 minutes.

Strain through a fine-mesh strainer, pressing with the back of a spoon to extract as much liquid as possible, and discard the solids. Add the sugar, vinegar, and citric acid and stir until fully dissolved. Store the shrub in an airtight container in the fridge for up to 1 week.

# CANDIED CRANBERRIES

Makes about 2 dozen candied cranberries

½ cup plus 1 tablespoon (112 g) sugar

¼ teaspoon vanilla extract

¼ teaspoon orange liqueur

1 dash coconut extract or almond extract

⅓ cup (30 g) fresh cranberries

Combine ½ cup (100 g) of the sugar, the vanilla, orange liqueur, and coconut extract, and ½ cup (120 ml) water in a small saucepan over medium heat. Cook, stirring occasionally, just until the sugar dissolves, about 5 minutes. (Do not let the mixture come to a boil or the berries may burst.)

Turn off the heat. Add the cranberries and stir until well coated. Place a small plate inside the saucepan to completely submerge the berries, then store the saucepan and its contents in the fridge for at least 6 hours or ideally overnight.

Strain through a fine-mesh strainer. (Save the syrup for another use; it will keep for up to 1 week in an airtight container in the fridge and is great on ice cream or mixed with soda water.) Transfer the cranberries to a small baking sheet in an even layer and sprinkle with the remaining sugar, using a spoon or chop stick to stir the cranberries and ensure an even coating.

Allow the berries to harden at room temperature overnight. Store them in an airtight container at room temperature for up to 1 week.

# GREAT PERSUADER

At first a simple fusion of cognac and Calvados, this cocktail was presented with a makeover after a suggestion, followed by some gentle persuasion, to introduce Japanese whiskey to the mix. And I'm so glad for it because the result is a supremely balanced drink. Plus, the plum garnish is so irresistible, you may just make a batch to enjoy on their own! For the best results, prepare the sugared plum garnish right before you plan to serve.—*Ginevra*

| | |
|---|---|
| 1 dash La Charlotte absinthe | 0.5 ounce (15 ml) Toutain Calvados |
| 1 ounce (30 ml) Suntory Toki whiskey | 0.5 ounce (15 ml) Spiced Plum Syrup |
| 0.5 ounce (15 ml) Brisson VS Cognac | 1 Spiced Sugar Plum slice, skewered |

Rinse or atomize (finely spray) a Nick and Nora glass with the absinthe. Chill the glass.

Add the whiskey, cognac, Calvados, and syrup to a mixing glass. Fill the glass with ice and stir until chilled, 8 to 10 seconds. Strain into the chilled glass. Garnish with the spiced plum slice.

## SPICED PLUM SYRUP

Makes about 1 cup (240 ml)

3 ripe plums, halved and pitted

6 cinnamon sticks

½ teaspoon allspice berries

½ whole nutmeg, cracked

1 cup (200 g) sugar

Preheat the oven to 300°F (150°C). Arrange the plums flesh-side up in a single layer in a deep casserole dish. Add the cinnamon, allspice, nutmeg, and 2 cups (480 ml) water. Cover the dish with foil and bake until the plums have broken down, about 90 minutes.

Remove from the oven and strain through a fine-mesh strainer, pressing on the solids with the back of a spoon to extract as much liquid as possible. Discard the solids. Add the sugar and stir until fully dissolved. Store the syrup in an airtight container in the fridge for up to 1 week.

# SPICED SUGAR PLUMS

Makes about 12 slices

¼ cup (50 g) sugar

¼ teaspoon ground nutmeg

¼ teaspoon ground allspice

¼ teaspoon ground cinnamon

1 ripe plum, pitted and cut into about 12 thin slices

2 tablespoons Spiced Plum Syrup

Combine the sugar, nutmeg, allspice, and cinnamon in a small bowl.

Dip the plum slices in a small bowl of the syrup, or use a pastry brush to evenly coat both sides.

Dredge both sides of the syrup-coated plum slices in the sugar mixture and set aside to use as a garnish. Store in an airtight container at room temperature and use within 24 hours.

# DEVILED KOHLRABI
## with Green Olives

Serves 6 to 8

One of my favorite dishes to make growing up was egg salad with green olives. I was inspired by a recipe I discovered in a kids' cookbook in my elementary school's library. Over the years, I've tweaked this recipe many times, first by adding a dash of curry powder and some fresh herbs to make it a little more sophisticated, then to make it vegan by replacing the eggs with tofu or, in this version, kohlrabi. But the flavors of the mustard, mayonnaise, and green olives take me right back to the original. Top this dish with store-bought seaweed caviar and enjoy it with some champagne when you're feeling fancy.—*Rich*

---

3 cups (400 g) peeled kohlrabi, cut into ½-inch (1.25 cm) cubes

1 Yukon Gold or other waxy potato, peeled and chopped into 1-inch (2.5 cm) cubes

1 cup (220 g) vegan mayonnaise

¼ cup (60 ml) sunflower or vegetable oil

¼ cup (60 g) Dijon mustard

¼ cup (60 g) minced celery

¼ cup (60 g) minced red onion

2 tablespoons minced green olives

1 tablespoon Old Bay seasoning

1 tablespoon nutritional yeast

¼ teaspoon turmeric

1 teaspoon pepper

Bring a large pot of salted water to a boil. Add the kohlrabi and potato and cook until tender, about 12 minutes. Drain and let cool completely.

In a large bowl, combine the kohlrabi and potato with the mayonnaise, oil, mustard, celery, onion, olives, Old Bay, nutritional yeast, turmeric, and pepper until the potato has broken down and slightly thickened the sauce (the kohlrabi should remain intact). Chill for at least 30 minutes before serving.

**PAIR WITH . . .** Bay Bae (page 152) to pay tribute to all things '70s.

# HICKORY-PECAN CARAMEL CORN

*Serves 6 to 8*

The best part of making your own caramel corn is that it is truly customizable, with as many mix-ins as you like, or opportunities to experiment with unusual flavors—like the hickory syrup used here. We source shagbark hickory syrup from Falling Bark Farm through a phenomenal co-op called Appalachian Mercantile. Maple syrup works great here, too, but with a sharper, more heavily spiced flavor profile, hickory makes exquisite caramel.—*Kate*

**3 tablespoons sunflower or vegetable oil**

**⅓ cup (60 g) popcorn kernels**

**1 cup (220 g) brown sugar**

**½ cup (110 g) vegan butter**

**⅓ cup (80 ml) hickory syrup**

**½ teaspoon salt**

**½ teaspoon vanilla extract**

**¼ teaspoon baking soda**

**1 cup (110 g) chopped pecans**

**½ teaspoon ground sage**

**½ teaspoon ground cardamom**

Preheat the oven to 350°F (180°C). Line a baking sheet with parchment paper.

Add the oil and popcorn kernels to a large pot over high heat and stir. Once the first kernel pops, about 3 minutes, cover the pot, reduce the heat to medium, and shake the pot gently to ensure even popping until it tapers down to about 1 pop every 5 seconds, about 3 minutes. Set the popcorn aside in a large bowl.

Combine the brown sugar, butter, hickory syrup, salt, and vanilla in a medium saucepan and melt over medium heat until the sauce comes to a boil. Reduce the heat to medium-low and allow the sauce to caramelize, about 5 minutes. To test the caramel for doneness, dip in a spoon and then, holding the spoon away from the heat, allow the caramel to drip off; the caramel is ready when it clings to the spoon. If it continues to drip, give it another 30 seconds of cooking.

Carefully stir in the baking soda. This will cause the caramel to bubble up dramatically, then quickly deflate. Continue cooking for 10 seconds, then remove the caramel from the heat and stir in the pecans, sage, and cardamom. Pour the caramel over the popcorn and stir to coat evenly.

Transfer the caramel corn to the prepared baking sheet and bake just until crispy, about 15 minutes. Let cool completely. Store in an airtight container at room temperature for up to 1 week.

**PAIR WITH . . .** a glass or two of **Bury the Hatchet** (page 162)—the cocktail's tartness is like the seasonal cherry on top of this sweet and salty snack!

# OLD ACQUAINTANCE

"Auld Lang Syne" is a festive and sentimental song that celebrates the end of another year and the friends and acquaintances who got us this far. So fill up your glass with smoky Scotch and floral orange essence, raise a toast to old friends, and sing along as the year wanes. Hardy oranges are a citrus fruit that ripens in our region during the late fall; their oily rinds are a key ingredient in oleo saccharum (literally "oily sugar"), a concentrated, aromatic syrup. If you can't find them, you can substitute half the amount of blood oranges or Mandarins.—*Kate*

**1 dash Laphroaig Scotch**

**1 ounce (30 ml) Famous Grouse Blended Scotch**

**0.5 ounce (15 ml) Cocchi Storico Vermouth di Torino**

**0.5 ounce (15 ml) Nardini Rabarbaro**

**0.5 ounce (15 ml) Dolin Génépi**

**1 teaspoon Hardy Orange Oleo Saccharum**

**1 dash Saline Solution (page 41)**

**Orange peel**

Rinse or atomize (lightly spray) a chilled coupe glass with the Laphroaig, discarding any excess.

Add the Famous Grouse, vermouth, rabarbaro, génépi, oleo saccharum, and saline solution to a mixing glass. Fill the glass with ice and stir until chilled, 8 to 10 seconds. Strain into the chilled glass. Garnish with the orange peel.

## HARDY ORANGE OLEO SACCHARUM

Makes about ½ cup (120 ml)

**12 hardy oranges (see Headnote)**

**½ cup (100 g) sugar**

Wearing latex gloves to keep your hands clean, carefully peel the oranges. Juice the oranges using a citrus juicer. Combine no more than 2 tablespoons of the juice with the peels in a medium bowl, add the sugar, and massage well to help extract the peels' oils, then cover the bowl and let rest in the fridge for at least 6 hours or ideally overnight.

Strain the mixture through a fine-mesh strainer, pressing on the solids with the back of a spoon to extract as much liquid as possible before discarding the solids. Store the oleo saccharum in an airtight container in the fridge for up to 5 days.

# MUSHROOM TAPENADE

## Serves 6 to 8

Inspired by the traditional tapenade spread of olives and capers from the south of France, we gave this dish a deep, meaty flavor by adding portobello mushrooms. The mushrooms' umami and silky texture work beautifully with the olives, both the fruity beldi and salty kalamata. Serve the tapenade with fresh or toasted baguette slices, some cashew cheese, and crudités.—*Rich*

---

**2 portobello mushrooms, chopped**

**¼ cup plus 1 tablespoon (75 ml) olive oil**

**½ teaspoon salt**

**1¼ teaspoon pepper**

**½ cup (60 g) oil-cured pitted Beldi olives**

**½ cup (60 g) pitted, chopped kalamata olives**

**¼ cup (30 g) capers, drained**

**2 tablespoons chopped shallot**

**1 tablespoon sherry vinegar**

**2 garlic cloves, chopped**

**1 tablespoon chopped fresh thyme**

Preheat the oven to 425°F (220°C). Line a baking sheet with parchment paper. Toss the mushrooms on the prepared baking sheet in 1 tablespoon of the olive oil, the salt, and ¼ teaspoon of the pepper, then roast until tender, about 15 minutes.

Let cool for a few minutes, then transfer to a food processor. Add the Beldi olives, kalamata olives, capers, shallot, vinegar, garlic, and thyme, and pulse until smooth. Serve.

**PAIR WITH . . . Beet Mind Eraser** (page 155). The sweet-and-sour beet cocktail is positively perfect with the earthy mushrooms and salty olives.

# POMEGRANATE BOULEVARDIER

The vermouth and pomegranate molasses are a perfect match in this delicately balanced boulevardier. When I first read about the technique of adding a couple grains of uncooked sushi rice to the mixing glass with the other ingredients to soften their astringency and help meld their flavors, I knew I had to try it out right away—and to my delight, it really works!—*Ginevra*

**1.5 ounces (45 ml) Rittenhouse Rye**

**0.75 ounce (22 ml) Campari**

**0.5 ounce (15 ml) Carpano Antica Formula Vermouth**

**0.5 ounce (15 ml) Pomegranate Molasses Syrup**

**8 grains sushi rice**

**Pomegranate seeds or orange twist**

Add the rye, Campari, vermouth, syrup, and rice to a mixing glass. Fill the glass with ice and stir until chilled, 8 to 10 seconds. Strain through a Hawthorne strainer held over a conical strainer into a double rocks glass with a large ice cube. Garnish with the pomegranate seeds.

## POMEGRANATE MOLASSES SYRUP

Makes about ½ cup (120 ml)

**¼ cup (60 ml) pomegranate molasses**

Bring ¼ cup (60 ml) water to a boil in a small saucepan over high heat. Remove from the heat and stir in the pomegranate molasses. Let cool completely, then store the syrup in an airtight container in the fridge for up to 1 week.

# WINTER

## Drinks

## Snacks

**E**verything you've heard about farm life is true. Lost Glove, our little farm in Chester County, Pennsylvania, is a ton of work, often met with frustration and disappointment, but the effort is ultimately redeemed by the glorious rewards of the harvest. You watch the weather like it's your job. You find yourself tuning into all the nuances of nature: the bugs and the birds, the clouds and the sun and the soil. Your senses are heightened as you become part of the ecosystem that you have created.

And as autumn color gives way to wintry chill, you are acutely aware of the fact that all this work, and all this life, is about to go to sleep. It's a realization that brings a simultaneous rush of sadness and relief. Soon it will be time to go inside, light a fire, and get to all those projects around the house that have been piling up for the last six months. Winter is the time for reading, writing, thinking, and dreaming. Time slows and you curl up in front of a movie with a really good bottle of red wine, resigned to the fact that the sun now sets at 4:30 PM and that spring feels an eon away.

## Winter is the time for reading, writing, thinking, and dreaming.

Winter's austerity presents a challenge in the kitchen, but it's also my favorite time to cook. There's no choice but to get creative. In the winter I crave deep, dark flavors: I caramelize my onions deeply, I deglaze with red wine or Madeira. I cook hardy root vegetables with dried sage and rosemary. I revel in thick, hearty stews. Our preserved ingredients and robust sauces are potions that will get us through the season.

By late February the housework is done, writings have been put to ink, the movie to-watch list is getting lean, and I'm starting to climb the walls. I've had enough cabernet; I want sunshine and a rum on the rocks. I can hear lapping waves calling to me from Caribbean shores. A three- or four-day reset somewhere warm—where the food is great and the tequila flows easy—revives me, but I am also reminded of the need to accept the cycle of life in the northeastern United States where we live. Its lush rolling hills, forests, lakes, and fertile soils make it impossible to ever leave. Just a little winter reset . . . that's all. Then we come home, back into the cycle of waiting, planning, and dreaming, as spring gets closer every single day.

—Rich

# HEADBANGER

When brainstorming names for this carroty drink, we toyed at first with references to everything from rabbits to eye charts—until the perfect name came to us courtesy of a character in Sir Terry Pratchett's Discworld fantasy series. In his youth, Carrot Ironfoundersson, a towering, red-haired member of the City Watch who was raised by dwarfs, would frequently knock his noggin on the low cave ceilings of his home, earning himself the nickname "Head-Banger." Naturally, we just had to name this luscious, brash, carrot-centric cocktail after our favorite city watchman. (What can we say? We're big nerds.)—*Brian*

**1 teaspoon maple syrup**

**1 teaspoon black and white sesame seeds, toasted**

**1½ ounces (45 ml) Libelula Joven tequila**

**1 ounce (30 ml) carrot juice**

**1 ounce (30 ml) Maple Tahini**

**0.5 ounce (15 ml) lemon juice**

**6 dashes Jerry Thomas' Own Decanter bitters**

**1 teaspoon aquafaba**

Brush the maple syrup down the side of a double rocks glass using a pastry brush, then roll the coated side in the sesame seeds.

Add the tequila, carrot juice, maple tahini, lemon juice, and bitters to a cocktail shaker. Fill the shaker with ice and shake vigorously for 8 to 10 seconds. Strain into the prepared glass with a large ice cube.

## MAPLE TAHINI
Makes about 1 cup (240 ml)

**2 tablespoons tahini**

**¼ cup (60 ml) Simple Syrup (page 10)**

**⅔ cup (160 ml) maple syrup**

**¼ teaspoon xanthan gum**

Add the tahini, simple syrup, maple syrup, and xanthan gum to a blender and blend on high speed for 1 minute. (The heat generated by the blending will help emulsify the mixture.) Store in an airtight container in the fridge for up to 1 week. Before using, let the mixture come to room temperature and whisk to recombine.

# CELERY ROOT RILLETTES

Serves 6 to 8

Our farm, Lost Glove, is a constant source of culinary inspiration. In the summer, it's buzzing with life, the scene for outdoor cocktail hours and sunset barbecues. Winter months are quieter. We find ourselves daydreaming about being in a cozy Provençal farmhouse, and this take on rillettes, the French classic, is the perfect snack to accompany a fireplace cocktail. At once rustic and elegant, the trick here is to pulse the celery root into a very coarse puree. This dish is best served with crackers or crostini, but French bread is also great. It also makes a good tea sandwich filling.—*Rich*

---

**4 cups (600 g) peeled and chopped celery root**

**¼ cup (60 ml) olive oil**

**1 teaspoon salt**

**2 teaspoons pepper**

**2 cups (440 g) vegan mayonnaise**

**½ cup (60 g) chopped celery**

**¼ cup (15 g) lightly packed tarragon leaves**

**¼ cup (15 g) lightly packed parsley**

**¼ cup (40 g) chopped cornichons**

**¼ cup (60 g) minced shallot**

**¼ cup (30 g) capers, drained**

**1 tablespoon Dijon mustard**

Preheat the oven to 400°F (200°C). Line a baking sheet with parchment paper.

Toss the celery root with the oil and salt and 1 teaspoon of the pepper. Transfer to the prepared baking sheet, place in the oven, and roast until the celery root is soft and golden on the edges, about 15 minutes. Remove from the oven and let cool for 15 minutes.

Transfer the roasted celery root to a food processor in 3 to 4 batches and process with an equal portion of the mayonnaise, celery, tarragon, parsley, cornichons, shallot, capers, mustard, and the remaining pepper, pulsing until the texture is a coarse and chunky puree.

Gently fold together all the batches and chill in the fridge for at least 20 minutes before serving.

**PAIR WITH...** a sophisticated cocktail like **Ginny's Freezer Martini** (page 185) to complement the briny and herbal high notes.

# GINNY'S FREEZER MARTINI

This drink is almost too good to be true. It makes a big batch that, once mixed, goes directly into your freezer to be enjoyed right out of the bottle whenever the mood strikes. You literally can't beat that! A balance of botanical and Plymouth-style gins, a yuzu curaçao liqueur, and vermouth blanc, it's a drink for an elegant party. Tonic bitters and orange blossom water add fragrant aromas that lift it perfectly.—*Ginevra*

**3 dashes tonic bitters**

**2 drops orange blossom water**

**3.75 ounces (110 ml) Batched Ginny's Freezer Martini**

**Cilantro flower**

Chill a coupe glass.

Add the bitters and orange blossom water to the chilled glass, then pour in the freezer martini. Garnish with the cilantro flower.

## BATCHED GINNY'S FREEZER MARTINI

Makes about 2 quarts (2 L)

**1½ cups (360 ml) Plymouth gin**

**1½ cups (360 ml) Uncle Val's Botanical Gin**

**1½ cups (360 ml) Dolin Blanc vermouth**

**1¼ cups plus 2 tablespoons (330 ml) Pierre Ferrand Yuzu Curaçao**

**1½ cups (360 ml) cold water**

Add the Plymouth gin, Uncle Val's gin, vermouth, curaçao, and cold water to a large, freezer-safe, airtight container. Stir to combine, then seal the container and freeze for at least 3 hours or ideally overnight. The cocktail mix can be stored in the freezer for up to 6 months.

# HEEBIE JEEBIE

Our nonalcoholic beverages are very important to our beverage program, and the Heebie Jeebie is always the most popular on the menu! Essentially a hibiscus lemonade with an electric magenta color, the drink is energized even further with the intense jolt of ginger. Factor in the lemon juice and this antioxidant refresher will keep you nice and healthy all winter long.—*Kate*

0.75 ounce (22 ml) Hibiscus Syrup

0.75 ounce (22 ml) Ginger Syrup (page 113)

0.5 ounce (15 ml) lemon juice

3 ounces (90 ml) soda water

Lemon wheel

Add the hibiscus syrup, ginger syrup, and lemon juice to a Collins glass. Top with the soda water, fill the glass with ice, and stir until chilled, 8 to 10 seconds. Garnish with the lemon wheel.

## HIBISCUS SYRUP

*Makes about 1 cup (120 ml)*

½ cup (100 g) sugar

3 dried hibiscus flowers (10 g)

Pinch of salt

Add the sugar, hibiscus flowers, salt, and ½ cup (120 ml) water to a small saucepan over medium heat and cook, stirring occasionally, until the sugar dissolves and the syrup is dark pink, about 5 minutes.

Strain through a fine-mesh strainer and discard the solids. Let cool completely before storing in an airtight container in the fridge for up to 5 days.

 **SPIKE IT**   Try adding 2 ounces (60 ml) of any light-colored spirit, like vodka, gin, or blanco tequila.

# WHITE SWEET POTATOES
## with Chimichurri

Serves 8

If you think you don't like sweet potatoes, chances are you're thinking of the orange-fleshed variety. From the Hayman potato to the Cuban boniato to the Japanese beni azuma, creamy-colored white sweet potatoes are nutty and only slightly sweet, and they make for a stick-to-your ribs winter snack. We coat them in chile butter, and all they need for balance is the lip-smacking sharpness of a chimichurri. We especially like to use Hayman sweet potatoes here.—*Rich*

---

**2 pounds (900 g) white sweet potatoes, cut into 1-inch (2.5 cm) rounds**

**½ cup plus 2 tablespoons (150 ml) olive oil**

**2 teaspoons salt**

**3 tablespoons vegan butter**

**1 tablespoon Aleppo chile powder**

**1 cup (60 g) lightly packed cilantro**

**1 cup (60 g) lightly packed parsley**

**½ cup (80 g) chopped white onion**

**¼ cup (60 ml) lime juice**

**3 garlic cloves, chopped**

**2 teaspoons red pepper flakes**

**2 teaspoons pepper**

**1 teaspoon rice wine vinegar**

Heat the oven to 400°F (200°C). Line a baking sheet with parchment paper.

Toss the potatoes in 2 tablespoons of the oil and 1 teaspoon of the salt. Transfer to the prepared baking sheet and roast until fork-tender and the skins begin to look wrinkled, 15 to 30 minutes depending on the size of the potatoes.

Transfer the potatoes to a large bowl with the butter and turn gently to coat evenly, sprinkling with the Aleppo chile powder as you turn them.

To make the chimichurri, add the cilantro, parsley, onion, lime juice, garlic cloves, red pepper flakes, pepper, vinegar, and the remaining oil and salt to a food processor and pulse until you have a chunky relish, about 1 minute.

To serve, pour the chimichurri onto a serving dish, spread into a thin layer, and then stack the potatoes in the center.

 **PAIR WITH . . . Headbanger** (page 181) to match the energy of this sweet, smoky, and sour small plate.

# DRIFTING SUNWARD

Like our houseplants bending toward the light or our cats chasing sunny spots for nap time, this cocktail is named for the wistful longing for sun many of us feel during the winter. An antidote to the winter blues, this vibrantly colored, sparkling cocktail is bold with a citrusy, herbal flavor. Any sparkling wine will do, but we like a Cava with powerful bubbles.—*Brian*

**1.5 ounces (45 ml) Poblano Tequila**

**1 ounce (30 ml) tangerine juice**

**0.75 ounce (22 ml) Chareau**

**0.5 ounce (15 ml) lime juice**

**0.25 ounce (7 ml) Simple Syrup (page 10)**

**2 ounces (60 ml) sparkling wine**

**Lime wedge**

Add tequila, tangerine juice, Chareau, lime juice, simple syrup, and sparkling wine to a Collins or wine glass. Fill the glass with ice and stir until chilled, 8 to 10 seconds. Garnish with the lime wedge.

## POBLANO TEQUILA

Makes about 2 cups (480 ml)

**½ fresh poblano chile, stemmed and seeded**

**¼ fresh serrano chile, stemmed and seeded**

**2 cups (480 ml) Rejon Blanco tequila**

Using tongs, hold the poblanos and serranos about 6 inches (15 cm) above an open flame (such as a gas stove burner) and toast them until their skins start to char all over, about 3 minutes. Alternatively, broil the chiles in the oven just until they start to char, about 3 minutes.

Let the chiles cool just enough to handle, then dice them and add to a jar with the tequila. Cover and let rest for 8 hours or ideally overnight.

Strain the mixture through a fine-mesh strainer, then discard the solids. Store in an airtight container for up to 1 week.

# CAULIFLOWER GRENOBLOISE

*Serves 4 to 6*

Grenobloise, a lemony caper sauce, deserves to have its moment. This French classic is often overlooked in favor of the more well-known beurre blanc and hollandaise, but in the dead of winter it adds a burst of sunshine. In fact, it's one of my go-tos for quick, easy, and sophisticated winter meals. This version makes for an ideal cocktail-friendly small plate when drizzled over nutty roasted cauliflower.—*Rich*

1 cauliflower head, cut into 2-inch (5 cm) florets

¼ cup (60 ml) olive oil

2 teaspoons salt

2 teaspoons pepper

¼ cup (60 g) minced shallot

2 garlic cloves, chopped

¼ cup (60 ml) white wine

1 cup (225 g) vegan butter, softened

¼ cup (60 g) Dijon mustard

½ cup (25 g) minced chives

⅓ cup (45 g) capers, drained

3 tablespoons lemon juice

1 tablespoon chopped tarragon

Preheat the oven to 400°F (200°C).

Toss the cauliflower in 2 tablespoons of the oil, 1 teaspoon of the salt, and 1 teaspoon of the pepper. Transfer the cauliflower to a baking sheet and roast until the edges start to brown, about 15 minutes.

Meanwhile, heat the remaining oil in a medium saucepan over medium heat. Add the shallot, garlic, and the remaining salt and pepper and cook until golden brown, about 3 minutes. Deglaze the pan with the wine and cook until reduced by half, 1 to 2 minutes. Remove from the heat and stir in the butter and mustard and ¼ cup (60 ml) water. Once the butter is melted, let the mixture cool for 10 minutes before stirring in the chives, capers, lemon juice, and tarragon. Transfer to a small bowl.

Arrange the roasted cauliflower on a serving dish and serve with the sauce.

**PAIR WITH . . . Drifting Sunward** (page 190) to blast away the winter blues with a double dose of citrus!

# COME MONDAY

Named after a Jimmy Buffett song, this drink is best enjoyed after the holiday rush, when all you're craving is the return to routine and simple home comforts. Part escapism and part seasonal celebration of winter citrus, this tropical-leaning drink is a sweet indulgence.—*Kate*

| | |
|---|---|
| 1 dash aged rum | 0.5 ounce (15 ml) Kumquat Syrup |
| 1.5 ounces (45 ml) Mount Gay rum | 0.5 ounce (15 ml) lime juice |
| 0.5 ounce (15 ml) Salers aperitif | Kumquat |

Rinse or atomize (lightly spray) a chilled Nick and Nora glass with the aged rum, discarding any extra.

Combine the Mount Gay rum, aperitif, syrup, and lime juice in a cocktail shaker. Fill the shaker with ice and shake for 8 to 10 seconds. Strain into the chilled glass.

Use a paring knife to slice an X into the skin on one end of the kumquat, then carefully peel the 4 corners back halfway to create a flower. Garnish the drink with the kumquat flower.

## KUMQUAT SYRUP

Makes about ½ cup (120 ml)

½ cup (115 g) chopped kumquats, seeded

½ cup (100 g) sugar

1 small star anise

Heat the kumquats, sugar, star anise, and ½ cup (120 ml) water in a medium saucepan over low heat just until the mixture comes to a boil. Reduce the heat to low and simmer until the kumquats are soft and translucent, about 10 minutes.

Remove the star anise and let the mixture cool completely, then blend until smooth. Strain through a fine-mesh strainer, pressing on the solids with the back of a spoon to extract as much liquid as possible, and discard the solids. Store the syrup in an airtight container in the fridge for up to 3 days.

# KNOCKOUT PUNCH

I owe this drink's creation to my friend Yvette, who upon hearing that I'd made a cinnamon-cardamom simple syrup instantly said, "Let's make a daiquiri with it!" and then, after taking a sip, "Let's make a milk punch!" Like the Ginny's Freezer Martini (page 185), this is a batch-ahead-and-enjoy-whenever cocktail—perfect for serving when you're hosting a party and don't want to be stuck behind the bar all night.—*Ginevra*

3 ounces (90 ml) Batched Knockout Punch

Dehydrated lime wheel

Pour the punch into a double rocks glass filled with ice. Garnish with the dehydrated lime wheel.

## BATCHED KNOCKOUT PUNCH

Makes about 1⅓ quarts (1.5 L)

1½ cups (360 ml) Flor de Cana Extra Seco rum

1 cup (240 ml) Smith & Cross rum

1 cup (240 ml) lime juice (about 8 limes)

1 cup (240 ml) coconut milk

1 recipe Cinnamon-Cardamom Syrup

½ cup (120 ml) Wray & Nephew rum

Combine the Flor de Cana rum, Smith & Cross rum, lime juice, coconut milk, syrup, and Wray & Nephew rum in an airtight container and allow to rest in the fridge for 8 hours or ideally overnight.

Clarify the mixture by straining it first through a fine-mesh strainer, then a cheesecloth, and then a coffee filter. (You could take a shortcut and strain the mixture only through the fine-mesh strainer, but you'll get the clearest results from the three-step filtering process.) Store the punch in an airtight container in the fridge for up to 2 weeks.

## CINNAMON-CARDAMOM SYRUP

Makes about 1 cup (240 ml)

1 cinnamon stick, crushed

2 cardamom pods, crushed

½ cup (100 g) sugar

Combine the cinnamon stick, cardamom, sugar, and ½ cup (120 ml) water in a small saucepan over medium heat and cook until the sugar dissolves, about 5 minutes. Remove from the heat and strain through a fine-mesh strainer, discarding the solids. Store the syrup in an airtight container in the fridge for up to 1 week.

# KUMQUAT BARS

Serves 8 to 10

Nothing perks up the post–holiday doldrums like the sunny flavors of citrus. Kumquats are floral and honeyed in flavor, with an edible rind that makes them a great fruit for both cocktails and candied fruit toppings. Paired with nutty frangipane and layered over flaky pastry, these bars are the perfect treat for a chilly afternoon.—*Kate*

### PASTRY

1¾ cups (220 g) flour

¾ teaspoon salt

1 teaspoon sugar

½ cup (110 g) cold vegan butter, cut into 1-inch (2.5 cm) slices

2 tablespoons olive oil

¼ cup (60 ml) ice-cold water

### FRANGIPANE

2 cups (240 g) roasted, salted, shelled pistachios

¾ cup (150 g) sugar

½ cup (110 g) vegan butter

⅓ cup (40 g) flour

¼ cup (35 g) tapioca starch

1 teaspoon lemon zest

¼ teaspoon salt

### KUMQUAT TOPPING

3 cups (690 g) kumquats (about 40 kumquats), seeded and thinly sliced

1½ cups (300 g) sugar

1 tablespoon lemon juice

To make the pastry dough, sift together the flour, salt, and sugar in a medium bowl. Using a dough cutter or fork, cut in the butter and oil just until crumbly. Drizzle in the cold water and gently mix to incorporate. Press the dough into a disk (the dough will be delicate and crumbly), wrap it tightly in plastic wrap, and refrigerate for at least 30 minutes.

To make the frangipane, while the dough chills, combine the pistachios, sugar, butter, flour, tapioca starch, lemon zest, salt, and ⅓ cup (80 ml) water in a food processor. Pulse until the mixture is smooth and creamy, about 1 minute.

Heat the oven to 350°F (180°C). Line a 9 x 13–inch (22 x 32 cm) baking dish with sides at least 1 inch (2.5 cm) high with parchment paper.

Lightly dust the counter with flour, then turn out the dough and use a rolling pin to roll it into a rectangle roughly the size of the baking dish. Transfer the dough to the prepared baking dish, poke all over with a fork to prevent bubbling, place in the oven, and bake the crust until golden brown, about 60 minutes.

To make the kumquat topping, while the crust bakes, combine the kumquats with the sugar and 1½ cups (360 ml) water in a medium saucepan over medium heat. Cook, stirring occasionally, until the syrup reduces in volume by half and the kumquats are soft, about 20 minutes. Remove from the heat and stir in the lemon juice.

Let the crust cool slightly, then spread the frangipane over it in an even layer. Top the frangipane layer with the kumquat topping, then return the pan to the oven and bake for another 15 minutes. Remove it from the oven, cut into 12 bars, and serve warm or at room temperature. Store in an airtight container at room temperature for up to 2 days or in the fridge for up to 1 week.

**PAIR WITH . . . Come Monday** (page 194) to use up an abundance of fresh kumquats in style.

# BERMUDA ROSE

This drink, our version of a Jack Rose, is a cocktail for lovers. We use hibiscus instead of grenadine for a touch of tartness, and we improvise further by adding a little Gosling's Black Seal rum and Kahlúa coffee liqueur. With a nice amount of fresh lime, it's sweet, but not saccharine—an excellent choice for Valentine's Day.—*Brian*

1 ounce (30 ml) Laird's apple brandy

1 ounce (30 ml) lime juice

0.5 ounce (15 ml) Gosling's
Black Seal rum

0.5 ounce (15 ml) Kahlúa

0.5 ounce (15 ml) Hibiscus Syrup
(page 186)

1 dash chocolate bitters

Chill a coupe glass.

Add the brandy, lime juice, rum, Kahlúa, syrup, and bitters to a cocktail shaker. Fill the shaker with ice and shake for 8 to 10 seconds. Strain into the chilled glass.

# MISS WORLDWIDE

If you like things a little spicy and funky, you're my kind of person—and this is your kind of cocktail. It's a complex tropical refresher, with tequila, lime, yuzu koshō (a tangy, spicy paste made from chile peppers and citrus peel), and passion fruit, and scented with a garnish of sprinkled Urfa pepper and beet powder. If you can't find Urfa pepper or beet powder, Aleppo pepper and rose powder make fine substitutes.—*Ginevra*

| | |
|---|---|
| Lime wheel | 2 ounces (60 ml) Libélula Joven tequila |
| Pinch of Urfa pepper powder (see headnote) | 0.75 ounce (22 ml) Passion Fruit–Yuzu Koshō Syrup |
| Pinch of beet powder | 0.5 ounce (15 ml) lime juice |

Lightly dust the lime wheel with the Urfa pepper and beet powders and set aside for garnishing.

Add the tequila, syrup, and lime juice to a cocktail shaker. Fill the shaker with ice and shake for 8 to 10 seconds. Strain into a Collins glass filled with fresh ice. Garnish with the lime wheel.

## PASSION FRUIT–YUZU KOSHŌ SYRUP

*Makes about 1½ cups (360 ml)*

1 cup (240 ml) passion fruit puree

⅓ cup (65 g) granulated sugar

2 tablespoons brown sugar

2 teaspoons yuzu koshō (see Headnote)

Combine the passion fruit, granulated sugar, brown sugar, yuzu koshō, and 2 tablespoons water in a blender and blend until the sugar is dissolved and the mixture is slightly frothy and lighter in color, 30 to 60 seconds. Store the syrup in an airtight container in the fridge for up to 5 days.

# PUB MIX

## Serves 6 to 8

Traditional British pubs are known the world over for their comfort food and bitter beers, perfect for all-day sipping. What might be surprising is that today these pubs are some of the world's most vegan-friendly drinking establishments, serving up dishes like plant-based bangers and mash and creative mushroom pies—as well as classics like this pub mix, perfect for crunching by the handful over a pint.—*Rich*

**2 cups (300 g) salted, roasted peanuts**

**2 cups (85 g) crunchy potato sticks**

**2 cups (180 g) corn nuts**

**2 cups (180 g) small pretzel sticks**

**2 teaspoons nutritional yeast**

**1 teaspoon dried ground sage**

**1 teaspoon pepper**

**¼ teaspoon dry mustard powder**

Combine the peanuts, potato sticks, corn nuts, pretzels, nutritional yeast, sage, pepper, and mustard powder in a large bowl. Store in an airtight container at room temperature for up to 1 week.

 **PAIR WITH...** **Knockout Punch** (page 197), which is just as good paired with these salty snacks from "down the local" as it is on a tropical vacation.

# PARTING WORDS

We joke that the work we do at Vedge is like throwing a dinner party every night, and when the nights go seamlessly, as they often do now that we've been at it for so many years, it doesn't feel like work. Sure, there's practice and planning and business stuff behind the scenes, but when we're immersed in service each night, we're in our element.

We hope the recipes in this book have shown you that your bar absolutely can be as exciting and creative as your kitchen. We hope they've motivated you to sling some new drinks, test out techniques, and experiment with ingredients you hadn't considered before; to dig deep into your CSA box, get creative with fruits and veggies, or consider reaching a little further back in your spice cabinet.

We also hope that, just as we delight in taking care of our customers throughout the year, you'll take pleasure in gathering to share a drink with friends and family. Maybe it's late winter, and you're hosting an intimate family-only dinner party. Perhaps you and your bestie are barbacking at a late summer barbecue. Or maybe you and a few family members are prepping snacks for a big holiday celebration. Whatever your reason for opening this book, we hope it serves as a catalyst for good food and drink and good conversation as you practice the art of hospitality, season after season.

—Kate and Rich

# ACKNOWLEDGMENTS

You're only as good as the team that surrounds you. And we have the most amazing teams, both at Vedge and in our personal lives: people who surround us with their talent and love and make a book like this possible.

First, we must give a shout-out to our staff at Vedge—the finest in Philadelphia! We are honored to work alongside you. Elpidio and Bernie, from helping us open back in 2011 to guiding us through the pandemic, you two are the heart and soul of Vedge. Amanda, you are one of the most dedicated, creative, and fearless leaders we have ever known; your helming the kitchen puts everyone at ease. Our current staff lineup is a terrific reflection of the Vedge ethos of loyalty, commitment, and pride in doing great work. Alex Jr., Alex Sr., Alex S., Alex U., Allison, Arnold, Berna, Colin, David, Ed, Emery, Enrique, Harry, Hugo, James, Jayna, Julie, Kenny, Kirsten, Maria, Meghan, Oliver, Rebecca, Robby, Rufino, Sergio, Yeni, and Yvette, you are all critical to the restaurant's success. And Ginevra and Brian, reading through your bar recipes crystallized our vision for this book. Your talent and deep understanding of cocktails are awe-inspiring, and the two of you have truly embraced and elevated Vedge's approach to our bar program. We are thrilled to have shared this effort with you.

To The Experiment, a huge thanks! To Matthew for discovering us over a decade ago, helping make the first Vedge cookbook a reality, and then continuing to believe in us. To Sara for your enthusiasm from day one, for tirelessly sifting through so many drafts, for all your queries, and for cheerfully keeping us organized. To Beth for a drop-dead gorgeous design that perfectly captures the sense of place and for managing our marathon photography sessions. And to Ally, Bessie, Margie, Jennifer, Kamryn, Pamela, Will, Zach, and all the other folks at The Experiment, we thank you for your support in making and promoting this book.

Ted, in many ways this book is your baby. With your eye, your angles, your willingness to crawl, tower over, reach around—whatever it took to get the perfect shot—you graciously took the lead on the photo shoot, and the results have left us all with dropped jaws. We are forever grateful to have fused our art with yours.

To our amazing crew (many of whom have been with us on and off for years) at Ground Provisions, Vedge's sister restaurant out in West Chester, Pennsylvania, you've helped us realize our longtime dream of connecting more closely with local farms, rolling up our sleeves, and digging in the dirt. Thank you for keeping things running so we could focus on this book, and for nurturing a seasonal sensibility that gets stronger with each growing cycle.

To our family and friends. You give us the social fuel and diversion so desperately needed to keep us out of our own heads and show us there is so much more to life than work—no matter how meaningful and fun the work is.

To our longtime patrons. Many of you have supported us for over two decades now, since even before we opened Vedge. Thank you for sticking with us through all these years and bearing witness to our evolution.

Finally, to our son, Rio, to whom the first Vedge cookbook is dedicated. We are so very proud of you and the beautiful human you've become. Working with you in the kitchen over the summer is always a thrill. There is a bond of love, support, and understanding between us that we will carry throughout our lives.

# INDEX

NOTE: Page references in *italics* refer to photos.

# ABOUT THE AUTHORS

**KATE JACOBY** is a CMS Certified Sommelier and James Beard Award–nominated pastry chef. With more than two decades of hospitality experience at the helm of Vedge Restaurant Group with her husband, Rich, she continues to enjoy the creative process and sharing her enthusiasm for natural wines and plant-based flavors with staff and guests. Outside the restaurant, if not traveling with Rich and their son, Rio, you'll find her digging in her organic garden, learning Chinese medicine, or walking rescue pups.

**CHEF RICHARD LANDAU** is a six-time James Beard Award finalist and has twice been named Best Chef in Philadelphia by *Philadelphia* magazine. A pioneer of plant-based fine dining, he loves being part of the restaurant's everyday operations and developing the menus with his chefs; menu-change day will always be his favorite. Traveling the world to eat and drink with wife, Kate, and son, Rio, is his other passion. When not in the restaurant, he can be found biking, golfing, and, yes, cooking.

⊙ chefrichardlandau

**BRIAN BOLLES** has been developing thoughtful cocktails for nearly twenty years at bars and restaurants in Chicago and Philadelphia. When not behind the bar at Vedge, he plays *Dungeons & Dragons*, board games, and hardcourt bike polo. He lives in Philadelphia with his wife and cat.

**GINEVRA REIFF** has more than a decade of experience working in bars and restaurants. Currently a senior bartender at Vedge, she has a passion for vegetable drink creation. Her cocktails are often inspired by her travels around the world to destinations including India, Italy, Israel, France, Aruba, and Morocco. She loves to learn new technical bar skills and to craft cocktails that inspire wonder and delight.